GOOD BROTHERS
LOOKING FOR
GOOD SISTERS

JAWANZA KUNJUFU

CHICAGO, ILLINOIS

TABLE OF CONTENTS

Preface

PREFACE

My earnest prayer is that you enjoy reading my first book of fiction as much as I enjoyed writing it. I love being an instrument for the Lord. Each year He has given me a book that was on the cutting edge of our society. I have no idea if I will ever write another book of fiction. The Lord will (through His many vehicles—and that includes the readers) let me know!

When I told my female friends (nationwide) that the title of my latest book, *Good Brothers Looking for Good Sisters*, they candidly responded with, "you darn right its fiction." I am very much aware of the male shortage, remember I'm the author of *Countering the Conspiracy to Destroy Black Boys* and *Adam! Where Are You?* But that does not negate the fact there are good brothers available and how some sisters are overlooking them.

God Bless You,

Jawanza

CHAPTER ONE

James

It's been a long day, and James is tired. Rubbing his eyes, he fights an overpowering urge to sleep. Through sheer effort of will, he stands and stretches to get the energy flowing, but his body does not respond. He's too tired. He rubs eyes that are burning from having stared into the blue and white light of the computer monitor for twelve hours straight.

The life of an accountant around tax time isn't easy. Only five more days until D-day, and the workload isn't about to get any lighter between now and April 15. It's a good problem for an entrepreneur, but still, the long hours have taken their toll and it's all James can do to stay awake. The garbage can under his desk is filled with white styrofoam cups colored with the stains of strong black coffee. Not even coffee can keep these eyes open, he thinks. If only there was some good woman standing behind him now, putting soft brown fingers to his temples, massaging the weariness out of his head.

He sighs. It's times like this, when he's alone late in his office after a long, hard day, when he feels the loneliness of being a bachelor most profoundly. The old, persistent desire for companionship, love, and support rises up within him like a powerful force, undeniable, especially when he has little energy to redirect his thoughts to work and more work. All he wants right now is the understanding of a special woman who supports him in what he's trying to do with his company.

Why else would he work so hard at being a success if not to share it all with a good woman? To raise a family and provide for wife and children? James sighs. He often wishes the desire would just go away and leave him alone.

After all, what woman wants a husband who's never home? James spends more time in the office than any other place on earth. Sometimes months go by before he remembers to call his mother, and he can't remember the last time he went to see a movie. What woman would tolerate that kind of a life?

No one on James' staff puts in longer hours or works harder than he does. James is driven by the need to become financially independent, but his commitment to excellence goes far beyond his immediate desire to make money. The Black community will regain its strength only to the extent that Black businesses are able to provide jobs and recycle the dollars currently gushing out of the community like blood from a gaping wound. Sometimes James feels like the last man in the world who cares about his community, but he refuses to give up.

He looks at his undergraduate degree, framed in gold, from Morehouse College. His Atlanta years were good ones, and he'll forever consider himself a Morehouse Man. Many of his friends feel the same way. He had to give it to his alma mater—Morehouse was a class act. From the intensive ten-day freshman orientation until the last day of graduation, the school takes care of its students and provides an education that rivals the ivy league colleges. Because of the school's supportive culture, James thrived, making the honor roll during his entire college career.

James' biggest challenge had been trying to find a sweetheart over at sister school Spelman College. He often complained to his parents about the difficulty of finding and falling in love with a Nubian queen, but they'd just smile knowingly and advise him to stop worrying and just enjoy college life—the classes, homecoming games, the Sweetheart Ball, and the occasional trips with the team. Love will come, they promised, in its own good time. Be patient, they said.

Patience. James stretches and sighs. Five years later, and he still isn't married. It's not that he doesn't know any women. He knows quite a few. But for one reason or another, the right situation has not materialized.

For example, he had really liked Paulette, a sister he met while still at Morehouse, but James wanted to secure his MBA in Pennsylvania and she wanted to teach in Mississippi. That was a big problem with college graduates. Who compromises when it comes time to decide where to live? Even questions like who will stay home with the children are now topics for debate and discussion. The stakes are higher when graduate degrees are involved. James stares at his MBA from Wharton, wondering if he'll have to be a monk for the rest of his life.

James' life isn't all longing, however. There are good times—the thrill of a job well done, the accomplishment he feels at the end of a productive day, and the signing of a new client really gets his adrenaline pumping. His hard work is beginning to pay off financially, too. His desk is made of real walnut. The carpeting in his office is a soft, tranquil ivory color. It feels thick and plush under his shoes. He knows he owes a great debt to the African American entrepreneurs who have gone before him reviewing income statements, balance sheets, bank reconciliations, cash flow statements, cost of goods sold statements, and stock portfolios, which is what he's done since day one.

On the wall next to his MBA from Wharton is James' Certified Public Accountant certificate. Of all the tests he had ever taken, that four-day exam was the hardest. It had taken him four attempts to pass the exam. He had sailed through the sections on taxes, theory, and auditing. It was that law section that brought him to his knees.

Recruiters at IBM made him an offer he couldn't refuse, so soon after graduation, he plunged into corporate life. As a $32,000 per year staff accountant, James was finally able to start paying back his student loans. He also opened a money market account with a financial planner (a fellow Morehouse Man), to which he contributed monthly. As for the job itself, the work was fulfilling and mentally stimulating, and the on-the-job experience he gained was great, but, as he was soon to discover, corporate life and a strong African American man were like oil and water. They just didn't mix.

Frustration at the glass ceiling soon led to resentment. He wanted more of the meaty tax work, but management had him typecast as a journeyman auditor. Him, a Morehouse Man, reduced to a mere numbers crunching. It was embarrassing.

Around the time when his resentment reached its peak, a co-worker named Denise entered his life. Also a CPA, Denise was funny, smart, and one fine woman. He enjoyed debating her on the intricacies of accounting theory, and he fell in love with her right in the middle of one such debate. Her brown eyes were flashing with a sexy self-righteousness. Her words were like a smouldering heat on his face. She leaned forward and jabbed his shoulder to make a point, and he felt a jolt of electricity. She felt it too, and smiled in surprise.

"What was that?" she whispered.

"I don't know, but you wanna have dinner Saturday?" he asked.

From that moment on, the two had been inseparable—for about a month. The relationship quickly soured as James began to realize, sorrowfully, that their values were too different to make a good match.

For example, even though their salaries were about the same, Denise never once offered to help with the check when they went out to lunch or dinner. James was so irritated by this that he talked to his sister Donna about it. "When you go out with your female friends, who pays?" he asked.

"We take turns," she said.

"How is it that when females go out together they take turns, but when a male and female go out together, it's understood that the male is going to foot the bill?"

"James, tell the truth. You would have thought your manhood was being challenged if Denise had offered to pay."

"Not true!" he said, although he suspected that she might be right.

James had other problems with Denise, too. When his White supervisor assigned James the task of training a new accountant, he was flattered until he found out through the grapevine that the guy was starting at $35,000. Same position. In fact, James had four years seniority on this guy, and he was only making $33,000. He was irate. That he had to train him just added insult to injury.

During this difficult time, he really needed to talk to Denise. He needed a sensitive and understanding ear. But for some reason he never got that from her. Denise would say things like "that's the male ego" or "you knew it was their company when you started." She would remind him of what Neely Fuller, Jr., said in *The United Independent Compensatory Code/System/Concept*: "If you do not understand White Supremacy (Racism)—what it is, and how it works—everything *else* that you understand will only confuse you."

"If you understand all that then how could you reduce my feelings to mere ego?" he asked. "The problem is, you don't understand. You don't *want* to understand."

"I understand that the Black man can't fight White supremacy by whining and pouting," she shouted. That hurt.

"Because it *is* a male thing *you* don't have to deal with it," he said angrily.

"I don't like the situation, but hey, they pay me well for the work I do. I give them a good eight hours and then I'm through for the day."

"So you plan to be here the rest of your life? You plan to slave away in the Big House until you retire?" James asked.

"Like I said, they pay me well. We have an agreement. I give them a good eight hours work and they give me a good eight hours pay. I don't have any illusions about being a department head, a vice president, or a CEO. I simply look at it as getting paid."

James shook his head in disgust. "Well, I can't deal with that. It's more than about getting paid to me. It's about justice. It's about what's right. It's about my manhood (that's different from ego). It's about racism. It's about them using me to train one of theirs to be my supervisor. How am I going to train someone to be my supervisor? That doesn't make any sense."

"Baby, relax. Just play the game," Denise said with those pretty light brown eyes and golden-peach skin.

"My days are numbered at this company. If they are paying me $33,000, I must be making at least $66,000 for them. I want to make that for myself."

"So you plan to leave this good job and start a business with no contracts, no office, no experience as an entrepreneur, with all the unemployed accountants and freelancers out there? You're going to be competing against established accounting firms. What's your niche going to be—Black companies? Black people don't want to pay Black professionals what they're worth. They'd prefer to take their business to the White man because we still believe they're the superior race. You must be crazy!" said Denise.

James stared at her. He couldn't believe what he was hearing. He abruptly stood up and walked out. The next day he called and apologized, however. Denise was polite, though cool. They went out to dinner later that evening to their favorite restaurant, which happened to be Black-owned and served the best French and soul food cuisine this side of the Mississippi.

"I can't live with you and I can't live without you," James said miserably. "You're so pretty, so smart, and you make me mad as hell. Denise, I want you to understand how I feel."

"No you don't. You want me to agree with you, and there's a difference."

"No I don't," said James. "I just want you to understand how I feel. If you understand how I feel, then you'll agree with me.

"Denise, I want to start my own accounting firm. I believe in myself, and I believe there's more to life than working for White people. If I gave forty years of my life to corporate America and didn't even try to make it on my own, I'd have regrets the rest of my life—and I'd resent you, too." Denise lowered her head. "Don't you ever think about starting your own business? Aren't you curious about what it would be like to go out on your own and write your own checks? After all, IBM started out as just a dream in the minds of a few people."

"I understand what you're saying," said Denise, "but I don't have that desire. I'm not a risk taker. I don't want that kind of stress in my life. I don't want to work twelve to fourteen hours a day and for less money. I'll admit that IBM is using me, but I'm using them, too. And so it's mutual.

"James, how many successful Black entrepreneurs do you know who are making over $50,000 a year, work only eight hours a day, are happily married, and are spending quality time with their children?"

"A lot!" said James. "I can't tell you whether they are happily married and how much quality time they spend with their children, but I do know that they're married and that they're in the *Black Enterprise* Top 100. But what if I didn't know of a soul? Why couldn't I be the first?"

"Realistically, James, most entrepreneurs are struggling. The long hours put a strain on marriages, and entrepreneurs *don't* spend enough time with their children. They can't."

"So, Denise, you would like for us to stay at IBM, continue to train less qualified White people to be our supervisors, at some point get married, combine our salaries to buy a house out in fantasyland, work eight hours a day, take one vacation a year to Hawaii, just the two of us, and another with our children to Disney World in Orlando?"

"Yeah, you got it. That's what I want and what's wrong with that?"

"As much as I want the vacations, the house, and all that, what I want more is to be financially self-sufficient. I have too much to just give away to IBM. I know that eventually, I'll be generating more money on my own. Denise, do you believe you could be married to an entrepreneur? Do you think that you could stay at IBM while I start my business?"

"Well, how much money do you plan to make the first year?" Denise asked.

"I can't tell you how much money I'll make or how many hours I'll have to work. I doubt I'll be making close to what I'm making now."

13

"So you propose to pimp me for a while and then leave me after I get yo' butt settled!" she teased.

"I'm serious! You think I'm joking about this. You may have to finance me at the beginning, but when yo' butt gets downsized, then you'll be running to me for a job. Maybe I'll hire you to type my letters."

"Sure," said Denise. "That'll be the day when you hire me." They looked at each other. All jokes aside, they both knew the end was in sight.

Just the memory of Denise makes James feel the sadness all over again. He looks around his office for comfort. Whatever happened to Denise? Maybe I should have married her. They would have made some pretty babies together. Maui would have been nice. Just the two of them, sitting on the beach, watching the sun set, eating mangoes and papayas.

Denise was right about one thing: being an entrepreneur was more than just a notion. Long hours. Financial uncertainty. Stress. But he knows, deep in his gut, that he made the right decision to leave IBM. It took him three years before he could afford his first administrative assistant, but now, with a staff of seven accountants, he's starting to get choice accounts. In the past few years, he's learned a lot, but the most important lesson he has learned is this: It's more rewarding to use your skills to become self-sufficient than allowing yourself to be pimped by corporate America and White supremacy.

The telephone rings. It's his current girlfriend, Carla. "James! Are you still at the office? How did I know you wouldn't be at home? It's 11:00 p.m. Are you planning to spend the night at the office? What are you going to do on April 15? Plan a sleepover? Have you ever heard of filing for an extension?"

James had to laugh. That woman had a serious mouth on her, but she was sweet. "What I like most about you, Carla, is that you can have a conversation without me. I promise you, I'm going home in a few minutes. I'm going to take a nice hot bath, drink some herbal tea, do my sit-ups, read a few scriptures, and go to bed." Carla sighed loudly. He could see her pouting. "Carla, I promise you that on April 16, I'll make it up to you. I'll take you to the best restaurant in the city. I'm going to wine and dine you and show you just how much I appreciate you. And just maybe, at some point (hopefully during this decade), you'll accept me as I am, a hardworking Black man who is looking for a good woman to understand me."

"Good night, baby," says Carla softly. "I'll be patient. Until the 16th, *peace.*"

CHAPTER TWO
David

David sits in the car outside the Jackie Robinson Elementary School. His son, David Jr., is in the first grade here, and he'll be bursting through the doors any minute now. As David waits, he reviews his TO DO list for the weekend. Tonight it's grocery shopping, then Chuck E Cheese for a Muppet show and video games. On Saturday, there's a PTA meeting, a visit to the laundromat, and choir rehearsal for David Jr. in the early evening. On Sunday, there's church and then the football game on TV.

David prepares himself for the bundle of energy who's about to take over his life for the rest of the weekend. Sometimes that boy just wears David out.

"Daddy needs his space for reflection," he often tells him. Inevitably Junior will ask, "What does the word *reflection* mean?"

"You know when your teacher wants you to put your head on the desk and be still for a few moments to listen to your heart beat?"

"Yes. When we're too noisy, she makes us do that. Daddy, is that why you need space for reflection, because sometimes you're too noisy?"

David smiles. "Sure, son, I'm too noisy." Junior can be a handful, but David loves being his father. He loves it when Junior asks him thousands of questions. That boy holds the world record in question asking, thinks David, which means he's going to have champion brains. Pretty soon he won't be able to answer his son's questions. Well, he'll just tell him the truth: he doesn't have all the answers!

Ms. Johnson, Junior's teacher, agreed that encouraging David to ask questions was important. "It's too bad," she said, "that as age increases, questions decrease for many children."

David Jr. was born six years ago, and his parents were thrilled about giving birth to their first child.

David and Patricia had a beautiful marriage that began with a close, loving relationship in high school. When David was having trouble with geometry, Patricia tutored. When Patricia needed help in chemistry, David reciprocated. They were one of the few couples who could say they went to the junior prom, senior prom, and five year reunion together. At the age of 23 they decided to marry.

Patricia was a fine sister and a born-again Christian. She had a radiance and a glow that drew people to her. She could turn any brother's head, yet she managed to remain humble. She loved working with children and was a Headstart teacher. She bonded with children easily and was looking forward to becoming a mother.

Every time David thinks about his Patricia, the grief becomes fresh all over again. Tears slowly fall down his face. How many times has he cried over the past six years? Why did she have to go? The day his life changed is burned in his memory forever. It was a chilly morning in October. The contractions had started, they were strong and hard, and he rushed Patricia to the hospital. David was an excellent coach, talking her through the pain, helping her with her breathing.

What had gone wrong? They had gone to Lamaze classes together, and she had faithfully kept every one of her prenatal appointments. He had been there with her every step of the way. In fact, he often joked that they would give birth together.

They planned, they did everything they were supposed to do, but ultimately, it didn't matter. There were complications, she was bleeding profusely, and she passed out from shock. David was frantic. Patricia was rushed to emergency, and David wasn't allowed inside the operating room. He was going crazy, pacing back and forth outside the door. He must have walked five miles, just pacing, back and forth. And praying. Would the tears never stop? Would it ever get easier?

After eight hours, Dr. Carson emerged from the operating room looking somber and tired. David rushed to him and asked, "Are they okay? Are they okay?" The doctor sighed, then put a hand on David's shoulder. He gently steered him to a chair and sat him down.

"We did everything we could," said Dr. Carson, taking the seat across from him. David's first thought was of Patricia's emotional and physical health. They had planned on having a big family. Would she want to try again after this?

"We did everything we could for *her*." Suddenly time stopped. The world spun around, and David gripped the arm rest on the chair to steady himself.

"Her?" asked David. *"Her?"*

"David, you are the father of a healthy seven-pound, six-ounce baby boy, but Patricia did not make it."

"Her?" David cried. He convulsed, and Dr. Carson just held on to him. People walking by seemed startled at seeing two Black men hugging and crying with one another.

"If only I had been there. We did everything together. If only I had been there," moaned David. He was inconsolable.

"I'm so sorry," said Dr. Carson. "We did everything we could."

"Did she say anything? Did she know that the baby was alive? Did she know that it was a boy?" asked David.

"Yes."

"What was the last thing she said? Did she say anything?" The pleading look in David's eyes was too much, even for a doctor who had seen much pain in his career.

"Your wife said, 'Tell David to take care of our son.' Those were her last words."

Bam! David is jolted back to the present by a knocking on the car window. "Daddy, Daddy, let me in!" Junior is shouting. The time has flown by. It is 3:15 p.m. already, and his precious bundle of energy is ready for the weekend. David quickly wipes his eyes, opens the car door, and hugs his son.

"What did you do in school today?" David asks, driving onto the street. Junior shows him a picture of a stick figure family, one boy, one man, and both are smiling.

"I drew this in school today."

"I don't have a pointed nose," says David.

"But, Daddy, that's the only kind of nose I can draw. It's a picture of a father and a little boy, and they are holding hands.

"Daddy, I'm the only boy in school that doesn't have a mommy. A whole lot of my friends have mommies. Daddy, how come most children have a daddy *or* a mommy? Why can't we have both?"

"You had the best mommy any little boy could have. You had a mommy who, just like Jesus, gave her life for you. She died so that you could live."

"I can't wait to see her in heaven. Daddy, are you sure that she's looking down and smiling at us? Are you sure that she knows everything we're saying to each other? Does she know what we're going to do this weekend?" David Jr. looks into the sky and asks, "How can she see us? The sky's so far away and the moon's even farther, and the sky's even farther than that. Where's heaven, Daddy? How far away is it?"

"Son, I know your mommy is looking out for us, but I don't know where heaven is. Do you think God has an address?"

For some reason the question tickles Junior. "Yeah, and He gets mail." They both laugh at that one.

"Son, God gave us the best mail system in all the universe. He gave us prayer. All we have to do is pray, and faster than the speed of light, God receives the message. In fact, He knows our prayers *before* we even think them. How's that for speedy delivery?"

"Wow!" says Junior as David pulls into a parking lot at the grocery store. "Hey, there's Ms. Johnson. Ms. Johnson!" Junior jumps out the car and shouts and waves.

Ms. Johnson walks over to the car. "Hello, David," she says, smiling at them both.

"Hi, Ms. Johnson. How are you?" asks David.

"I'm blessed," she says.

"Praise God," says David.

"David Jr. did a good job in school today. You're doing a great job with the boy, Mr. Johnson. I know being a single parent is not easy, but he's going to be fine," says Ms. Johnson. "He's one of my top students." Junior beams.

"Thank you," says David.

"Did you show your dad the picture you drew in class today?"

"Yes, I showed it to him. You want to see it again?"

He goes into the car, and while he's searching for his work of art, Ms. Johnson says, "You should see some of the family pictures I get, Mr. Johnson. They could break your heart. One little girl drew herself as a dot with big scary monsters all around."

24

"God help her."

"I called the child welfare agency."

"Good!" says David. Junior jumps out of the car.

"I found it!" He waves his drawing in their faces.
"See?" he says excitedly.

"David Jr.!"

"I'm sorry. See?" he says, more subdued.

David takes the paper from him and shows it to Ms. Johnson. "See?"

"I see! I see!" laughs Ms. Johnson. "I see a happy, healthy family," she says, more for David's benefit than Junior's. David smiles and mouths a silent "thank you."

"So what are your plans for the weekend?" asks Ms. Johnson.

"We have a busy weekend," says David. "Grocery shopping, Chuck E Cheese, the laundromat, Jr. Rites of Passage program, choir rehearsal, and then we'll end the weekend on Sunday in church, praising the name of our Lord and Savior Jesus Christ."

"Sounds like a lot of fun. I only hope that David Jr. has time to do his homework. He has some math problems to do, and don't forget to study your new spelling words for the week. David Jr., what did you get on your spelling test today?" asks Ms. Johnson.

"I got a 95. I only missed one word!" says Junior excitedly. David roughs up his hair. Junior is so proud of himself he can barely contain himself.

"You two take care of each other and, God willing, we'll see each other on Monday morning. Toodleloo!"

"Toodleloo?" Junior asks David. Then, waving, he says, "Toodleloo!" David laughs. That boy cracks him up sometimes. "So now I know what we're doing this weekend," says David Jr. "We have a lot of things to do. What are we going to buy at the grocery store, Daddy?"

"Vegetables, fruit, and beans. Some juice. A lot of stuff. C'mon."

"Can I push the cart?" asks Junior. He wants to play and make the automatic doors open and close, but David gently shoves him inside.

"Yes, just remember that it's not a go-cart. You can't go racing up and down the aisles. We have to be respectful of everyone in the store, and we can't mess up the store's property," says David.

Since David and David Jr. are vegetarians, they spend most of their time in the produce section. "Daddy, can we get some grapes? I love grapes."

"Do you want the red or the green?" asks David.

"Can we have both? I like both kinds."

David weighs two pounds of each, along with oranges, apples, bananas, peaches, cantaloupe, watermelon, lettuce, tomatoes, and cucumbers.

"I can't wait until I get as tall as you, Daddy, so that I can pick up the watermelon," says Junior as he watches his father load the watermelon into the basket. "It's almost as big as I am."

David just smiles at Junior. "Time will come quick enough when you'll be able to pick up the watermelon and everything else in the basket because you're going to be strong. Look at gorillas. They're vegetarians, they love bananas, and look how strong they are."

David points Junior to the aisles that carry bread, beans, and rice. "You're doing a good job of pushing the cart. I think I'll make you the official cart pusher in the family. How'd you like that?"

"Wow!" says Junior. It never ceases to amaze David at how little it takes to build up a child's self-esteem.

They fill up the cart and head for the checkout line. Just in front of them is a cute, petite Black woman with carrot-colored skin and shoulder length braids. She peeks into their cart and says, "Hey! No meat! Are you guys vegetarians too?" David Jr. smirks. Even at six years old he's aware of women's attraction to his father. Wherever they go, it never fails, some woman will act interested in his daddy and start a conversation.

"Yes, and I can tell by the color of your skin that your favorite food is orange—carrots maybe?" asks David.

"I juice quite a bit."

"I've gotten lazy about juicing at home, so I cheat and buy what I need at the health food store."

"Well, you two have a nice weekend." She smiles and waves flirtatiously as she pays the cashier. As she walks away with her bag, David looks after her admiringly.

"Daddy, why are you looking at that lady like that? Do you want to marry her?"

David laughs. "Whoa! I was looking at her because she's pretty." Junior frowns. "Girls are not pretty. They're a pain." David chuckles. "Believe me, one day you'll understand. C'mon, boy, let's go."

As they walk out of the store, David hands one of the smaller bags to Junior so he can feel like he's helping. They put the groceries in the car, and David Jr. tells his father all about his day, starting with his spelling test, followed by reading, math, recess, science, lunch, Black history, and art. The details take a long time to tell. He's still talking when they reach the apartment.

"Did you learn a lot?" asks David.

"Yes, Daddy," says Junior, putting the celery in the refrigerator vegetable bin.

"What was the best thing you learned in school today?" asks David as he puts in the rest of the vegetables. He thinks he might make a big pot of vegetable stew later—after Chuck E Cheese.

"The best thing I learned today was this: I learned about a Black scientist named George Washington Carver. Daddy, if George Washington Carver invented peanut butter from the peanut, then why isn't *his* name on the jar of peanut butter?"

"Son of mine, that's the best question you've asked all day. Here's my answer: In Africa, when a great scientist invented or discovered something, it was to help everyone in the village. In America, if someone invents something, it's to make money."

Junior is very quiet. David knows that his words are stewing around in that fertile brain of his. More questions are sure to come at some time in the not too distant future, if he knows his son. And he does.

"Play with your toys until we're ready to go."

"Okay, Daddy. Can I watch TV?"

"Don't even think about it."

"Okay." Junior skips into his bedroom, off to the land of magic and adventure. David goes into his bedroom to check his messages.

David pushes the playback button, and his on-again, off-again girlfriend, Diane, says in a real sexy voice, "Hi, David. What are *we* doing this evening? What are *we* doing this weekend? I'm getting off work in about an hour and I would love to spend some quality time with my man—just me and you."

Before David can push the stop button, the phone rings. It's Diane. "Did you get my message?"

"Baby, you have amazing timing. We just walked in."

"So what do you think of my desires? Just you and me tonight. You can drop David Jr. off at your parents' house. They get to spend quality time with their grandson, and I get a chance to spend quality time with his father."

David is very quiet. This is just the reason why they are on again and off again. "Diane, I told you on Monday that I was taking Junior to Chuck E Cheese today."

"But you've packed your whole weekend with the father-son thing. Where do I fit in?" she asks.

"Diane, why does it just have to be you and me? How come *we* can't spend time with you? I'm just one man, and you're forcing me to choose between you and my son. That's not fair. What's the problem, Diane? Don't you like David Jr.?"

"Of course I like Junior. Sweet boy. It's just that I want to spend romantic time with you. Alone."

"We could be romantic at Chuck E Cheese. We could be romantic at the laundromat. And we could hold hands in church on Sunday. You're always welcome to join us. We *want* you to come."

"I know, David."

"Diane, I get the feeling that you don't like my package deal, but that's what Junior and I are."

31

"I just thought you would appreciate your lover calling you on a Friday evening with an irresistible invitation. Most men would."

"First of all, I'm not most men, and second of all, you know I love spending time with you. I just don't like the way you make things either/or. I shouldn't have to choose."

"David, two weeks ago the three of us went on a picnic together. Last month we went to the zoo. But, baby, let's get real. Grown-ups need to be alone sometimes."

"Well, my offer still stands. We're going to Chuck E Cheese in about half an hour. I can swing by and pick you up and we can all go together. How does that sound?" asks David.

After a long pause, Diane says, "I'll take a raincheck, David. Maybe we can hook up later this weekend."

David sighs. "Fine," he says, the disappointment obvious in his voice.

"Ciao," says Diane.

David is still holding the receiver when Junior runs into his room. "Daddy, what shirt can I wear?

The Michael Jordan shirt or the Malcolm X shirt?"
David is still thinking about the conversation with
Diane. "Daddy! Did you hear me? What shirt can I
wear? Michael Jordan or Malcolm X?"

"Sorry, son. My mind was a thousand miles away.
Which shirt to wear? Now, let's see. What does
Michael Jordan do?"

"Play basketball."

"What about Malcolm X? What did he do?"

"Didn't he get killed?" asks Junior.

"Yes, but what did he do?"

"Didn't he talk a lot to Black people?"

"Yes, he did. Why did he do that?"

"To help us think better? To help us live better?"

"Good answer! Now, who's done more for Black
people—Michael Jordan or Malcolm X?" Junior
holds up the Malcolm X shirt. "Then that's the one
you should wear."

"Okay," says Junior, and he skips back to his
room.

During the drive to Chuck E Cheese, David plays
back his conversation with Diane. He wonders if he

made the right decision. A noisy evening at Chuck E Cheese or a nice, quiet evening with Diane, listening to Baby Face and Toni Braxton. Truth is, he'd *prefer* to spend time with Diane. She is sensuous, beautiful, and warm. On the other hand, time with Junior is constant motion and a question a minute. No time out for the old and weary. How long will he be able to keep Diane while making David Jr. the priority?

He looks over at Junior whose current objects of fascination are the windshield wipers. It's raining and he's entranced by their ability to flick the rain from the windshield. He remembers Patricia's last words: "Tell David to take care of our son."

His life is sure different from his parents. He'd never planned to be a single parent, but here he was, raising a boy the best he could all by himself. If he could be half as good as his father had been with him, Junior would be okay. His father, who worked on the General Motors assembly line, had attended all of his track meets, debate tournaments, and choir concerts. His mother was always there too, but having his father show his love in this way made him feel so special.

Once he asked his father why he spent so much time with him. Many of his friends' fathers were absent or came by only occasionally. His father told him, "There is nothing more rewarding than being a father." David promised his father that he would try to be just as good when he became a father. Why couldn't Diane appreciate that?

It's a typical Friday evening crowd at Chuck E Cheese: large, noisy, and wild. David orders pizza and buys five dollars worth of coins so that Junior can play video games. David quickly grabs an empty table and waits for the pizza while Junior plays. As always, the place is filled with Black women and their children, but no men. David is an anomaly. He stands out because he's one of the few Black men there, and the only Black man by himself.

David feels the women's eyes on him. He smiles at some, but mostly keeps his focus on Junior. The older kids can get too wild because they usually have not been trained to look out for the younger children. When the veggie pizza is ready, David shouts and waves over the noise for Junior to come on and eat.

Excitedly Junior runs to the table, plops down, and grabs a slice of pizza.

"David Jr.! You know better!"

"I'm sorry, Daddy. I forgot." They place their palms together and say, "Thank you Lord for this day. Thank you for the food we're about to eat. We pray that it strengthens our body for Jesus' sake. Amen."

Watching Junior eat with such pleasure lets David know he's made the right decision. This is where he wants to be, with his son. He gave his word, and because he didn't go back on his promise, his son is happy. As enticing as Diane could be, this time with his son was too precious and more rewarding.

On the drive home, Junior falls asleep. David chuckles to himself. He wore himself out, he thinks. Me too. When they get to the apartment, David wakes Junior up.

"We're home, sleepyhead."

"Daddy, would you carry me? I'm sleepy."

"You weren't sleepy when you were singing with the Muppets. You weren't sleepy when you were playing Ninja Turtles. Just Ninja yourself up the stairs and into your pajamas and go to bed."

Junior grumbles and whines, but hushes quickly when David gives him that "don't try it" look.

As Junior changes into his pajamas, David looks at a picture of Diane on the mantle. She is one of the finest sisters David has ever seen. Her eyes, her nose, her lips, her complexion, her hair—it's all good. He checks the answering machine, hoping for a message from her. He's disappointed, but not surprised, that there is no message.

"I'm ready, Daddy," Junior calls. Resigned, David goes to tuck his son in for the night. "Would you read me a story, Daddy?"

"Sure. Which one?"

"The chicken and the eagle."

"Again? You've heard that story a hundred times."

"It's my favorite! It's funny how the eagle thinks he's a chicken and acts like a chicken. Do the chicken sound, Daddy."

"Quack, quack," says David dryly.

"That's not a chicken. That's a duck!" They both laugh.

"Okay, settle down." David tucks him in and Junior stares at his father wide-eyed. Junior falls asleep halfway through the story.

David turns off the light even though Junior likes to keep it on. He'll never know now that he's in never-never land, thinks David.

All that weekend, as David and Junior go about their chores and errands, he hopes that Diane will call and say, "Baby, it really doesn't matter what we do as long as we do it together. Even though I can think of three better places to be with you than the laundromat, rites of passage, and choir rehearsal, I can think of no better person to be with."

The phone call never comes.

CHAPTER THREE

Randolph

Randolph has the sensation that he is floating alone in a sea of White faces. They're all around him, staring at him as if he's some sort of exotic creature. Maybe he is. At Northwestern University, one of the top universities in the country and a member of the prestigious Big Ten Conference, he is one of the less than five percent of African Americans to graduate—and he knows of only two others who are receiving their bachelor's in engineering with him. He's the only one to graduate magna cum laude.

As he stares out over that foamy white sea, he hopes to find at least two Black faces that he knows in the crowd, his mother and father. Although they expected nothing less from him, he knows they are proud. He knows his mom brags about him incessantly at church. Randolph represents the third generation of college graduates in a family of master's degrees and Ph.D.'s. Never before had he felt such gratitude toward his parents for constantly pushing him to achieve. Had it not been for his parents and teachers, he knows he would not be here this afternoon. He would have to find a special way to thank them.

Randolph has made it in one of the toughest schools in the country. His love of math and science earned him his top grades and attracted the attention of a Fortune 500 company who offered him a starting salary of $45,000 as a chemical engineer. But, as he thinks back to grammar school and high school, that same love of math and science is what separated him from most of his classmates.

As the names are read of graduates from the Biology Department, an experience he had in the sixth grade suddenly comes to mind. There were approximately thirty students in his class, fifteen boys and fifteen girls. Three of the more popular girls, Kathy, Denise, and Pat, were also the prettiest girls in the class. They were cheerleaders, teachers' pets, and felt they had the power to "rank" the brothers.

Randolph once told his mother that he wished Kathy, Denise, or Pat would like him. "How do you know that they don't like you?" she asked.

"Because they always call me a nerd. Why aren't they called nerds? They get good grades." Why wouldn't one of the smartest girls in class choose him, one of the smartest boys? It was a great mystery that would haunt him, even throughout his college years. Popular girls would inevitably choose popular boys, like athletes.

It didn't matter that Randolph ranked all those brothers on math and spelling exams—they were handsome and could play basketball better than he could. They could fight better than he could. They talked back to the teacher. They wore the latest clothes. They also knew the latest dance steps. Randolph was average looking and on the chubby side. Randolph's mother used to tell him all the time that while men and women look at the *outside*, God looks at the *heart*. Randolph knew that his mother meant well, but she just didn't understand what it was like to be a smart Black boy in sixth grade.

Randolph remembers asking Marcus, one of the popular boys, to teach him how to play basketball, and in return he would help Marcus with fractions and percentages. Marcus turned out to be a bad basketball tutor, because to this day, Randolph still can't play basketball.

Randolph used to tell his mother how frustrated he was that he never learned how to play basketball. He thought he was abnormal. It seemed that everyone in the Black community could play basketball and dance, neither of which Randolph could do. Because dancing and basketball were used as standards for Blackness, Randolph began to wonder if he was truly Black.

Randolph remembers the day he threatened to secede from the Black race altogether. He couldn't play ball, he couldn't dance. Classmates called him names like "nerd," "white-acting," and "gay," and all because he stayed on the honor roll. What was the use of trying to be Black? What did it mean to be

Black? This became the second, and most important, great mystery of his young life.

As Randolph sits on the stage at his graduation, he wonders where Lamont, Donald, and Marcus are now. Are they graduating from a top institution magna cum laude? And whatever happened to Kathy, Denise, and Pat? Would they want to be with him now, or would they still rank him on how well he plays basketball or dances?

Karen, a graduating senior in the English department, catches his eye. She smiles, then quickly turns away. Every brother on campus wanted to hook up with Karen. She's fine and has a sweet personality, basically. As a cheerleader, she was one of the most popular African American women on campus.

When Karen was a freshman and was dating a senior on the basketball team, she could barely say hi and bye to Randolph. He'd invite her to study with him, but her answer was always "thanks but no thanks." He'd ask her out to art exhibits or the museum, but she was always too busy getting her hair or nails done, hanging out with her girlfriends, or spending time with some athlete or fraternity brother.

Fraternities. If his social life wasn't dry enough, his lack of fraternal affiliation made his isolation complete. In high school, the major criterion for hooking up with a fine sister was how well you could play basketball or dance. In college, fraternal affiliation was the new requirement for social acceptance. Sisters like watching the brothers step. Randolph learned that much of the conversation among Black students focused on parties, step shows, bid whist and spades games. Randolph had hoped that there would be a higher level of conversation among college students. More than once over the past four years he longed for stimulating conversation outside of class. Randolph finally came to the conclusion that there wasn't much difference among Black students in high school, college, and on the streets.

After being rejected so many times by Karen and other sisters, Randolph started going out with White girls. Nothing ticked Randolph off more than sisters who would see him with a White girl and say, "Oh, so I'm not good enough for you!" Randolph wanted to tell them, "You can't say nothin' to me 'cause when I wanted to be with you, you never had the time."

Randolph toyed with the idea of putting an ad in the *Daily Northwestern*:

> **SBM looking for SBF.**
>
> **Can you THINK? Call me! Please!**

After a while, Randolph stopped caring what people thought about him. They were going to think what they wanted to think. Well, real men *do* eat quiche, and real men *do* go to art galleries and museums, and if Black people had a problem with that, *tough!*

When Dennis Rodman was interviewed on *Oprah,* he said that he didn't have time for Black women now because when he was poor and a nobody, Black women would not give him the time of day. Now he doesn't have any time to give to them. When he was a nobody, White girls at least were respectful. Many Black women said that Rodman must be really naive if he thought White women were interested in him as a person. Didn't he know they only cared about his money?

Black women have a lot of nerve getting mad at his relationships with White girls, thinks Randolph. Black women date White men. Why would they get on his case for dating White women? His prefer-ence was for Black women, but if none would give him the time of day, what was he supposed to do? Study all the time?

What does it mean to be Black? wonders Randolph.

I don't want to be Black if I can't be me. I don't want to be Black if I can't be a scholar. I don't want to be Black if I have to speak Black English. I don't want to be Black if I can only major in the social sciences and not in math and science. I don't want to be Black if the only sport I'm allowed to play is basketball. I don't want to be Black if I have to accept that swimming, tennis, golf, and skiing are only for White people. Who made that up? Who wrote the Black Constitution that restricts what I can and cannot do? Why is it that families in Iowa and Wisconsin can get up at 5:00 a.m. and drive into Chicago to visit our museums and other cul-tural institutions, and here we are, practically next door to them, and you can't pay us to go?

Randolph's life review rolls out before him like the graduate procession. He waves to his parents, and they wave joyfully back. This is such a great day.

A couple of months ago, Karen called him up, asking him to tutor her in statistics. It took Karen four years to respond to his request to study together. If they had studied together from the beginning, thinks Randolph, they both would be graduating magna cum laude.

"Karen, why did it take you so long to accept my invitation to study together?" he asked her flat out. "All I ever wanted was to spend time with you. Even with what I knew about you, I still cared about you."

"What do you know? Who's been talking about me?" she asked nervously.

"I know that you took off that semester to have an abortion. That brother on the basketball team got you pregnant."

The color drained from her face, and what was left was a cold dread. "How did you know that?" she asked quietly.

"Girl, everybody knew. It was the talk of the locker rooms. You don't know how athletes, frat brothers, and the rank and file brothers on campus talk about you and the other sisters. They make bets on who will get you into bed first. You're like horses to them. Karen, that brother who got you pregnant?

He didn't love you. He was one of the main ones talking about you."

"I never loved him!" Karen shouted, tears running down her pretty face. She didn't want to cry, Randolph could tell, but she couldn't help it.

"I never said that you did," said Randolph gently. "Why did you sleep with him if you didn't love him?"

"What does love have to do with anything?" she asked angrily.

Randolph wondered if she still had feelings for the guy. He looked down at the books. "Let's just study," he said.

Then Karen did something that totally surprised him. She placed her slender hand over his. Thinking about it now, he could still feel the warmth. But there was also a feeling of urgency, desperation. "I've changed, Randolph. I'm not like I used to be. It's true that hooking up with Fred wasn't the smartest thing I could have done, but I was new to Northwestern and I wanted to fit in. I got instant status with that dog."

"Karen, I couldn't have given you status, but I would have given you love and anything I had to give. And I would never have taken advantage of you."

"Oh, Randolph," she sighed.

"We could have done so much together."

"Yeah, but back then, I wasn't into studying, going to operas, plays, art galleries, and all that stuff."

"All what stuff?" asked Randolph.

"You know what I mean."

"You mean all that *White* stuff? You know, I don't understand how Black people can go to Northwestern, which is virtually an all White school, and resent the fact that it revolves around White activities and a Eurocentric academic approach. In fact, I don't see us majoring in African American studies. And you know what is really embarrassing? White students outperforming African American students who can talk that Black stuff but can't get a decent grade. Maybe that's White acting, too—getting an A in an African American studies class," said Randolph angrily.

Karen removed her hand and stared at Randolph. "Do you want to be Black? Do you like being Black? Do you want to date a sister? Is it true that you really only like White girls?"

Randolph stares at her. "Why would you ask that, Karen?"

"You just seem angry at Black people. You think that you're better than us, don't you?"

"No, Karen, I don't feel that I am better than you or anybody else."

"But do you want to be Black?"

"Of course I do, but what does it mean to be Black?" asked Randolph.

"Are you on some mission to change the way Black people think? You don't think we're going to give up playing basketball and dancing anytime soon do you? Everybody can't graduate magna cum laude from Northwestern University in the Engineering Department, and if that's your definition of Blackness, you've just eliminated most of us from the race. Randolph, do you feel that you have to reach down to us, or do you want us to reach up to you?"

"Karen, don't you feel embarrassed when Whites think you are a beneficiary of some affirmative action quota rather than a true scholar? Didn't you feel embarrassed when *The Bell Curve* set out to prove us genetically inferior? Why do only forty percent of us graduate from college? Why are we are the only race that has more sisters graduating than brothers?"

"Randolph, sometimes you are just too deep and serious. I definitely need for you to tutor me in statistics because I really do not understand it and I cannot graduate without it, but I've got to ask you—do you ever lighten up and just relax? What do you do to relax? See, Black folks know how to relax. We're not going to commit suicide if we flunk out of Northwestern."

"Karen, why is it that with Black people, class topics are confined to in-class discussion? How come we can't talk philosophy over breakfast, statistics over lunch, and physics over dinner?"

"There you go getting deep again. Look, I don't like statistics, and the only reason why I'm taking it is because it's a requirement for graduation."

"Statistics is fascinating. Look at how politicians manipulate them to win elections! But, okay, skip statistics. How about English—that's your major. How come, in four years, we've never talked about Toni Morrison, Langston Hughes, Zora Neale Hurston, or any other Black writer? You have not shared one paper you have written with me."

"Sure, let's talk about *Their Eyes Were Watching God*," she said in a dry, bored voice.

51

"Best romantic novel ever written. I loved how Zora placed the love story within the broader social context. But while I'm on a roll, let me ask you this: Why didn't you want to study with me when we were freshmen? How come you didn't talk to me when you got in trouble? You knew I cared about you. I would have done anything for you.

"And how come, Karen, you did not dispute that lie that I only like White girls when you know I've been begging you to go out with me for four years? You could have told your girls the truth.

"And another thing: Were you really busy when I'd ask you out? Or was it that you just didn't want to go with me?"

"I told you I was immature as an underclassman. I thought it was positive to go with somebody on the basketball team or from Omega Psi Phi."

Randolph shook his head. "Answer me this: Why are you with me now? You could have gone to anybody in the math department to tutor you in statistics. Why wait until our senior year for us to get together? Be honest, Karen. Did you hear that starting July 1, I'll be working for Motorola as a Chemical Engineer making $45,000 a year?"

Karen's eyes flashed angrily. "I resent your implication."

"Do you deny it?"

"You're paranoid! I don't care about your salary."

"Be honest, Karen. Did you know I was going to make that kind of money when I graduated?"

"Yeah, I had heard that you had been given some very serious offers and I am happy for you. But you act like I'm going on welfare or something. After graduation, I may teach for a year or two or secure a job at a newspaper or a magazine. I may even pursue a master's degree in journalism. I haven't decided yet. I can take care of myself. I don't need a man to pay my bills." Randolph couldn't tell if she was truly offended or just playing the game.

"Karen, if I asked you to go with me to the Planetarium and the Aquarium in Chicago this weekend, be honest, what would you say?"

"I would say yes."

"Why wouldn't you go out with me when I was a mere nerd of an engineering student? I'm the same person, except for the fact that I'll soon be earning $45,000 a year."

"You are so incredibly arrogant!" shouted Karen. She started to gather up her books.

"Have you really matured in these four years, or are you talking to me because Fred didn't go pro? He didn't graduate either, did he? Or is it because the "Q" brother dropped out? You think I'll make a nice, convenient meal ticket, don't you?"

Karen slapped Randolph. "I hate you!"

"The truth hurts, doesn't it?" he said. "But you know, Karen, I've been getting slapped ever since I was in sixth grade. All I've ever wanted was a sister to appreciate me for who I am—an average looking brother who can think better than he can bounce a basketball and can analyze better than he can dance. You sisters want us to pity you because of the male shortage, but you contribute to your own downfall when you fail to encourage brothers to value academics."

"Randolph, I'm sorry you feel that way about sisters. Does that mean you'll continue to date White?"

Enraged, Randolph grabbed Karen's hand. "The truth hurts, doesn't it?" she shouted.

Randolph is startled as the president of Northwestern says, "Randolph Brown, magna cum laude,

Engineering Department." Randolph didn't realize that the time had gone by so fast. As he walks across that stage to receive the degree he has worked so hard for, he looks over at the English Department and wonders if he and Karen will ever understand each other.

CHAPTER FOUR

Ron

Ron glances at his watch—he's right on schedule. He double-parks in front of the Ace Hardware on Western Avenue and grabs a couple of boxes from the back of the truck. The weight might have made a weaker man tremble, but Ron is strong and in good shape. The brother can bench-press 420 pounds and not break a sweat. Tall with a muscular build, his chocolate brown skin and easy smile make older women long for their youth and younger women weak at the knees. He is what the sisters call *too fine*.

"Ron!" says Mr. Harvey, the owner. "How you be, bro?"

"Just fine, Mr. Harvey. Got a couple of boxes for you. Sign right here, please." While Mr. Harvey is signing, Ron is silently calculating the time it's going to take to get to his next destination on 35th and Martin Luther King Drive.

Ron bids Mr. Harvey a good afternoon and walks out to his truck. He is stopped by a sister with long red braids.

"Ooo, men in uniform are so sexy!" she says. She pulls a card out of her purse. "Call me." She walks away slowly, deliberately.

"Scandalous!" Ron thinks, but can't help smiling. The sisters sure aren't shy. Actually, he's surprised, not because she approached him—women do that all the time—but because she approached him while he was in his UPS uniform. Usually, when sisters find out he's a blue-collar worker, they turn cold. Maybe he'd give this one a call, he thinks as he watches her switch down the street.

At twenty-six years old, Ron is single and gainfully employed. He's worked at UPS for four years. In fact, his supervisor assigned him to one of the most demanding routes because of his longevity with the company and his consistent performance. Turn-over on this particular route had been atrocious. In the past two years, eight drivers had been assigned to the route; all of them either quit or requested transfers to quieter, more residential areas where the packages delivered were fewer and lighter. Ron doesn't mind the hard work, but he does feel UPS should pay him more. Four years ago he started at $9.50 per hour. Today he earns $12.85.

Driving out into the street, Ron reflects on the many places he has been today. Paint stores, hardware stores, florists, medical and dental offices, office supply stores, bookstores, schools, and a host of independent businesses specializing in real estate, insurance, accounting, and computer programming. Everyone on the route likes Ron, and favorite customers like Mr. Harvey know him by name.

Ron especially enjoys the route during the Christmas holidays because his customers tip so well. He learned back in the days when he delivered newspapers that extra effort pays off. Normally he would just throw the newspapers on the porch steps, but on Christmas day, he'd deliver them right into his customers' hands. "Merry Christmas," he'd say cheerfully, and most customers, unable to resist the charms of a hard-working, good-looking Black boy, would usually respond with a generous tip. On one Christmas he collected more than $500. Not bad for a teenager. Ten years later, he's doing the same thing. Today his customers give him money or company products such as flowers and wine. One accountant offered to do his tax returns for free. Ron vows that he will be a UPS driver for the rest of his life or until his muscles begin to atrophy.

After he has emptied his truck of all packages, he heads back to the warehouse. He enjoys the sensation of being high off the road. He feels in complete command of traffic. He knows it is childish, but he imagines that he is the master of the streets. It's his playful spirit that makes him a favorite Cub Scout leader among the boys of Troop 445. In fact, he's got a Cub Scout meeting tonight, and if he doesn't hurry up, he's going to be late. To make the meeting on time, he'll have to change into his uniform in the men's locker room. He wants to give his boys the same opportunity he had when he was a Scout to earn patches and learn valuable lessons. He steps on the gas.

When he finally gets to the warehouse, there is a line of trucks waiting to file inside and park. The big door of the warehouse rolls open, and Ron drives inside. The building is huge, about 500,000 square feet, and accommodates 100 trucks. Following behind Ron are ten more trucks. Interesting how the brothers who can never get to work on time are never late returning to the warehouse in time for the next shift.

Spirits are high as the brothers park their trucks. TGIF! they shout as they file in to clock out and collect their checks. Louis actually falls on his knees and loudly praises God. The brothers laugh and walk around him. "Louis, man, you ain't got no sense," says Ron.

"Hey, bro, I know where my blessings come from!"

"Let the party begin!" shouts another. Sisters wondering where to find Black men working need look no further than their local UPS warehouse at quitting time. No shortage of Black men there!

The problem with the search-and-find expedition of most Black women is that they're looking in all the wrong places. Downtown office buildings, from

Manhattan to L.A., are where large numbers of Black *women* work, not men.

"How was the route today?" asks Mr. Mitchell, the shift supervisor, as he gives Ron his check. Ron takes his check absentmindedly. He's more concerned about making the Cub Scout meeting on time.

"It was good, no problems," says Ron.

"Get some rest over the weekend, young man, because we need you bright and early on Monday morning."

"Have I ever missed a Monday, Mr. Mitchell?"

"No, I can't say that you have, Ron." Curbing absenteeism on Monday mornings is Mr. Mitchell's greatest challenge as a supervisor. He doesn't know if the problem is caused by hangovers or because checks have already been handed out on Friday. He has considered changing payroll to another day—maybe Tuesday or Wednesday—to help prevent no-shows on the two most critical volume days of the week, Monday and Friday.

Ron and Steve, another driver, take their checks and head for the locker room to change. "What are your plans for the weekend?" asks Ron.

"Well, tonight me and my lady will sip on some coolers, play a little Toni Braxton and Baby Face, then lay in each other's arms for the rest of the evening. What about you, homeboy? What's up with you?"

"I got Cub Scouts tonight, my mom's house tomorrow morning, the health club tomorrow afternoon, maybe a club Saturday night, and church on Sunday, praising my Lord and Savior Jesus Christ."

Steve stares at Ron as if he's some strange alien creature. He jerks his body up straight and gives him a salute. "I guess a man's gotta do what a man's gotta do. Step lightly, Black man," says Steve.

"Peace," says Ron.

Ron hurries to his jeep and heads for the church in his neighborhood where they hold the meetings. The other two men who promised to serve as Scout leaders have been inconsistent in their attendance. One is a banker and the other sells real estate. Sometimes Ron wonders why they agreed to be Cub Scout leaders in the first place. They never seem to have time to work with the youth, although they've been loud in their opinions about what needs to be done to curb problems like youth violence and substance abuse. Not only that, whenever Harold or Robert do come, they act as if they're doing the boys a favor.

Ron is always the first to arrive and the last to leave. "Once a Scout, always a Scout," he had been taught as a boy. Harold and Robert had been Boy Scouts too, but they must have missed that lesson. Ron thinks that the reason for their low level of motivation has to do with the fact that they're not saved. It's obvious they haven't read the Scriptures, "To whom much is given, much is also required" and "What you do unto the least of these you also do unto me."

As he drives to the church, Ron goes over the lessons he would like to cover tonight—CPR training and building model cars. The boys have been wanting to build model cars for awhile now. He remembers the thrill of building model cars with his father. They'd work all weekend figuring, fixing, and decorating.

Model cars it is, but he'd start with a lesson on CPR since that's a life and death issue. Save the fun stuff for last, and he'd have their attention for the entire evening.

Ron drives into the parking lot of his church. Trinity United Church of Christ, which is pastored by Dr. Jeremiah A. Wright, Jr., has more than seventy ministries, twenty of which are geared toward young people. It is a well-balanced church, consisting of middle-and lower-class men and women, young and old. When Nelson Mandela had been in jail, a Free South Africa sign stood boldly on the front lawn. In addition to the Black history and culture classes for children and adults, the church offers an HIV-AIDS ministry and economic development programs, including a credit union and an employment ministry. Pastor Wright preaches three sermons on Sunday and more than twenty Bible classes are taught during the week.

In many churches the pastor has a lightening bug personality where the light must always shine on them. Pastor Wright's visionary leadership empowers other people to lead ministries. Ron feels important and empowered by Pastor Wright. He takes pride in his Cub Scout ministry, and he takes his work seriously. He knows that for many of his boys, he might be the only responsible Black man they'll see all week.

Ron makes it to the Cub Scout meeting room with five minutes to spare. Four of the boys are already waiting on him.

Now that Ron is here, two of the mothers stand up to leave. As they gather their purses, Brenda says, "Hi, Ron. Harold and Robert haven't made it yet. Are they still in the program? We haven't seen them lately."

"I'm sure they're on their way. At least I hope so," says Ron.

As more mothers greet Ron and drop off their sons, he wonders where all the fathers are. Of the thirty-five boys in his troop, only two have fathers in the home, and they are not involved in the program. No need for brothers to go to clubs hunting for women. They were all here, dropping their boys off at Cub Scouts. And most of these mothers were probably available.

He had thought about asking one of the sisters out once. Carol was pretty and her son was always neat, clean, and well behaved. She was obviously a good mother. Yet, his attempts at small talk always ended in an uncomfortable silence. Ron noticed, however, that when Harold or Robert showed up, she lit up, talking a mile a minute. Most of the mothers did.

At first Ron just chalked it up to bad chemistry. But when it happened with two other women, he began to wonder what was really going on. Was it his looks? Did he have bad breath? He didn't think so. He keeps his body in good shape and he knows his face is pleasing to women. Then it hit him. The mothers had been warm to him—until that day when he had rushed to the meeting in his UPS uniform. He hadn't had time to change. Those mothers were actually looking down on him! He was there every week, taking care of *their* sons, but his dedication didn't matter. They preferred white-collar brothers who failed to meet their responsibilities.

At first it hurt him when he would overhear the sisters making plans with Harold and Robert to go to some club. Not once had they ever invited him to go with them. He would have liked to have gone with them, but he didn't have the right corporate pedigree. That African Americans were so entranced by titles appalled him. He was a hardworking brother getting a consistent paycheck that was more than enough to satisfy his needs. What more did they want?

"Okay, boys, line up and repeat the Cub Scout pledge after me," says Ron.

Aaron blurts out, "Where's Mr. Jones and Mr. Johnson?"

"I don't know, Aaron, but the show must go on. Line up and repeat after me."

• • •

Ron's mother is half his size, and to hug and kiss her son, she must rise up on her toes and stretch. "Ronnie! Baby!" she says. "Want some pancakes?"

"You know I do," he smiles, "with a big glass of milk." It is clear where Ron gets his good looks. Mrs. Brooks was cute when she was younger, but over the years, she has grown beautiful. Before he died, Ron's father would tell anyone who would listen that he was married to the finest woman on the planet. She would blush and tell him to stop, but he'd go on and on about her flawless dark skin, captivating smile, big hips (she'd hit him at point), and tiny waist. And she could cook too. Mr. Brooks had known heaven on earth, and that's what Ron wanted—heaven on earth in the arms of a fine woman who could cook.

There is a picture of his mother and father on the mantle. His father died two months before their thirtieth wedding anniversary. Ron still feels his father's presence strongly—it's as if he never went away. Ron sometimes catches his mother looking off into space or longingly at her favorite picture of them together. He worries about her, which is why he comes over so much.

Ron's father was a strong Black man who had worked at the main post office downtown. Ron missed their crazy arguments on which institution was the best—the post office or UPS. "For $3.00, the post office can deliver a package in two to three days. UPS will charge you $6.00." Mr. Brooks would say. Ron would laugh. "We deliver in two days, not two to three. Our customers also get proof of delivery immediately via our computer system, 'cause we're high tech. The post office is still using the horse and buggy system. That's why it takes so long to get the mail. You got to pray when you send your mail through the post office," said Ron. Mrs. Brooks would hush their foolishness with bribes of her famous peach cobbler or sweet potato pie. Once the ambrosia passed their lips, the two would forget what they had been fussing about and sit eating happily, totally pacified.

Mr. Brooks also led a troop of Cub Scouts on the weekends, even while working a full-time evening shift during the week at the post office. Every night for 18 years, Ron got a call from his father at 8:00 p.m. He could set his clock by that call. He wanted to know all about Ron's day at school, whether he had finished his homework and his chores, and if he was minding his mother. A man is only as good as his word, Ron's father used to say, and it was his father's model of consistency and stability that taught him how to be a man.

Ron never heard his father say anything negative about his wife. He never hit or cursed her. Theirs was a good marriage. He treated her like a queen. Even though Ron comes over as often as he can to visit his mother, he knows he'll never be able to match the love and support that his father provided her. All he can do is try, and he knows she is appreciative of his efforts.

If only his father had gotten regular checkups as his mother begged him to. He claimed he was the perfect picture of health. When the pains of prostate cancer became too great to ignore and he finally did go to the doctor, the cancer had metastasized throughout his body. The doctors gave him six months to live, if they were lucky. He died in five. Ron vowed he wouldn't go out that way, that he would exercise on a regular basis and get annual checkups. Early detection could have saved his father's life, and that hurt them even more. If only his dad hadn't been so stubborn he'd be here today, arguing the superiority of the U.S. postal system.

"Ronnie, the pancakes are ready," his mother calls from the kitchen.

Ron sneaks up behind her, kisses her on the cheek, then sits down at the kitchen table. "You're not going to eat anything?"

"No, baby, I'll just sit here and watch you eat. I may have a glass of orange juice."

"Mama, what else do you need me to do beside cutting the grass?" asks Ron.

She thinks a minute. "The basement door squeaks. Maybe it needs a new hinge or a good oiling." Ron nods and dives into the thick homemade pancakes. He smacks his lips in sheer delight.

"Ronnie, when are you going to get married and give me some grandbabbies that I can spoil rotten while I'm still on this earth?"

Ron laughs. "You ask me this question every time I come over here. The problem is I just can't find anyone as good as you. There's no sense in me marrying someone who pales in comparison to my mama."

She blushes prettily, the way she used to do when his father would sing her praises. "Oh, hush! How're the pancakes?"

"Too good! Mama, they don't make women like they used to. I'm not looking for much. I just want my woman to be fine and cook like you do. That's not too much to ask, is it?"

"No, baby, it's not, but maybe you're too picky. So what if she can't cook like me! I didn't start out making perfect pancakes and roasts. It took time and patience. Look for a willing spirit, honey child. That's more important than a woman who can throw down in the kitchen. If she's willing, I'll teach her what I know, so hurry up, okay? You're my one and only, so I'm counting on you."

"The pressure's on!" Ron laughs. He kisses her on the cheek and puts his dishes in the sink. "Let me go cut the grass, Grandma."

"I love the sound of that word. Call me that from now on."

Later that evening, Ron decides to go to a club after all. Maybe his mom is right. Maybe he's been too picky. With hope in his heart, a rhythm to his step, and smelling good in Grey Flannel cologne, he goes to the Clique. It's a buppie crowd, so he wears his black designer suit and a purple mandarin shirt with a thin gold chain around his neck. His black shoes are so shiny he can see himself and, if he might say so himself, he looks good.

The air at the club is smoky, and the mood is lively. The crowd has just gotten started. Maxwell is playing, "You're the highest of the high." He wonders why Maxwell didn't call it that rather than "Ascension" because he never says that word in the song. So Ron has renamed it "You're the highest of the high" and he feels that way tonight.

He can feel the eyes of several sisters upon him and the subsequent shifting of positions of the brothers. The staking out of territory is a man thing, and Ron knows how to play the game. He has his own methods for working the room. The best place to stand is near the ladies rest room because a brother can scope all the sisters.

Ron thinks, if only sisters knew why brothers stand near the rest room and that the best place to meet a brother is at the bar or close to the dance floor. Brothers hate going deep into the crowd looking for a dance partner.

"Good evening," says Ron to a sister walking out of the ladies room. He nods and smiles at several more, all of whom smile back flirtatiously. Tonight is going to be the night, sooky, sooky, thinks Ron happily.

Toni Braxton's latest song is playing, and Ron goes over to a table where two sisters are sitting. One is popping gum, which turns him off immediately. Gum popping makes women look immature, unsophisticated, and downright ugly. He asks the other sister to dance. She's dark and is wearing a simple red dress that accentuates her curves. Her hair is cut and styled short, like Halle Berry's. The gum popper rolls her eyes at him, while the dark lovely eyes him up and down in that bold way of sisters. He passes her first test, she smiles, and he escorts her out to the dance floor. She moves with a sensual subtlety, and Ron decides he's going to keep her out on the floor for as many songs as she'll allow. With every cut played by R. Kelly, Baby Face, Jodeci, and Anita, Ron steps up the conversation.

"So, what's your name?" he asks.

"Renee. Yours?"

"Ron. Do you come here often, Renee?" asks Ron. Not the most suave dialogue, but it's a start.

"I usually pass through every other weekend," says Renee. "What about you?"

"About the same. Sometimes I go to the Godfather or the Riviera. You really look good in that red dress," he says, reaching for her hand.

"Is that why you asked me to dance?" She doesn't refuse his hand. This is going well, he thinks.

"No, I asked you because I wanted to get to know you better." A Tupac tune steps up the beat. She slips her hand out of his. Was that rejection? he wonders. "Do you like rap music?" Ron asks.

"I like some of it. It's too bad what happened to Tupac," she says.

They're shouting over the music, and with the bass in the sound system, it's hard to hear each other. He concentrates on dancing for a while. He wants to show Renee how good he is on the floor. After dancing to Mary J. Blige, Ron escorts Renee to an empty table.

"How come I've never seen you here before?" asks Renee.

"I don't know, but I'm glad we met tonight. Maybe it's fate. Maybe it's our destiny. Maybe tonight was the night we were supposed to meet each other," says Ron. "Is your girlfriend going to be okay with you over here talking to me?"

"Thank you for asking, but she knows that a girl's gotta do what a girl's gotta do. We didn't come here to be with each other." Ron nods. "What kind of work do you do?" asks Renee.

Oh, no! The conversation had been going so well. Why did she have to go there? Ron's heart sank. He had been dreading that question, but he knew it would come at some point. He hated "the question." He never asked women that question. He really didn't care where and if they worked. As long as a sister was fine, had a sweet spirit, and could cook, or at least be willing to learn, that's what was important to him.

Ron doesn't want to answer her because he knows what her reaction will be. One time he lied to a sister and said he worked at UPS as an account executive. She was interested, but he never called her back, partly because he had been deeply ashamed of himself—he had let desperation get the best of him—and mostly because he did not want to be with someone he had to lie to. Ron is tempted to lie to Renee, but he goes ahead and tells her the truth.

"I'm a driver for UPS."

At first Renee merely shifts in her seat and tilts her head. Ron has a glimmer of hope. Then she says in a dry, monotone voice, "That's nice. How long have you been doing that?"

"About four years," he says, watching her intently. He's not ashamed of what he does, but he can see that she has a problem with it. There are a few awkward moments of the two sitting and listening to the music, neither one saying a word. Finally, Ron asks, "What kind of work do you do, Renee?"

"I'm a district manager for Xerox." Ron regrets that he even asked.

After a few more unbearable moments of silence, Ron offers to buy Renee a drink.

"Thanks, but no thanks." Ron understands that she's not just refusing the drink, but that he's been given his cue to beat it. Renee reaches over to shake his hand. "It was nice meeting you." Then she stands up and returns to the gum popper. Ron sadly watches them rake him over the coals. They are laughing and looking at him.

As Whitney sings to him and him alone about love and hope and sadness, he thinks about Renee and sisters like her who won't give a hardworking brother a break. He tries to tell himself that he could care less, but he's too honest to believe that lie. He cares, and the constant rejection hurts.

He thinks that maybe the club scene isn't for him, but how does a good brother go about finding a good sister? Would he ever find a woman with whom he could share his life? Would he ever enjoy the kind of marriage his parents shared? Would he ever be able to fulfill his mother's dream—and his own—of having children?

Ron buttons up his jacket and drives the long way home. How does a good brother go about finding a good sister?

CHAPTER FIVE

Sinclair

"Girl, he gave you *what?*"

Sabrina is nonchalantly holding a dozen roses in one hand and the phone in the other. "Sinclair is always buying me something. If it's not flowers one week, it's candy the next. He sends cards, he calls me at work just to see how I'm doing, he offers to help around the house or do errands. He's always there for me."

"So what are you complaining about? Do you think he's got some ulterior motive, like getting you into bed?"

"Do you know he has not even tried?" says Sabrina.

"You know that's got to come sooner or later. You gonna do it?"

"I don't know, girl."

"Why not? You're not a virgin," says Doris.

"Neither are you," says Sabrina.

"Yeah, but we're talking about you. You've gone to bed with other brothers. Why not Sinclair? He's much nicer than anybody else you've been with."

"Like I said, he hasn't even asked me. Even if he did, I don't know if I'd *want* to do the wild thang with him."

"Why not?"

"Girl, I don't know. He's just not my type."

"You don't know what you want."

"And you do?"

"I know this much: if a man bought me flowers, candy, cards, called me, and did all the things Sinclair does for you, I'd be doing everything I possibly could to stay with him," says Doris.

Sabrina sighs impatiently. "You're not in this, Doris. It's easy to talk about what you would do when you're on the outside looking in."

"Maybe so, but some things are obvious, like the way Tyrone treated you. Everybody but you know that he was dogging you out."

"What're you talking about?" asks Sabrina.

"Sabrina, I don't believe you. You still refuse to see the light," says Doris. "All those times you were sitting around waiting for him to call. Remember when he got fired from that job and you were giving him money? Do you like the way he talks to you?"

"How do you know how he talks to me? Are you there for every conversation?" asks Sabrina.

"Don't get mad at me, you know I'm your girl, but you're forgetting all the things you told me about him."

"Doris, you weren't there when he whispered sweet things in my ear. You weren't there when he told me how good I looked. You weren't there when we made love to each other and he told me he would never leave."

"Where is he now?" asks Doris.

"That's none of your business," snaps Sabrina.

"Why you calling me then?"

Sabrina's call waiting clicks. "I'm sorry, girl. You're right. Can you hold on just a minute?"

Sabrina clicks over and, just as she suspected, it's Sinclair on the other line. Her heart sinks. She wanted it to be Tyrone. "Hi, Sabrina, did you get my package today?" he asks.

"Yes, Sinclair," she says. "Hold on one second and let me clear the line." Sabrina clicks back to Doris. "Girl, I got to go. It's Mr. Sinclair on the phone."

"Now you be nice to him," says Doris. "A good man is hard to find."

Sabrina laughs and says, "You got that right." She clicks back over to Sinclair. "Thank you very much for the flowers, but you didn't have to do that."

"I know, but I wanted to. Don't you know that I want to spend the rest of my life with you? The flowers may die in a few days, but my love for you is eternal."

Corny, but sweet, she thinks. "Sinclair, how can say you love me when we haven't even made love to each other?"

"Don't you know, woman, that when I sent you the flowers I was making love to you? When I went to the supermarket and the cleaners for your mother,

I was making love to you. When I washed and waxed your car, I was making love to you."

"Why do you do those things, Sinclair?"

"Because I love you, Sabrina."

"But I don't do anything for you."

"That's true, you don't. How come?" asks Sinclair.

"I don't know. I guess because I've been hurt."

"I could make you love again," says Sinclair. "Do you think you'll be able to trust a man again?"

"Maybe. When I meet Mr. Right."

"Do you think you could be talking to Mr. Right right now?"

"You sure are asking a lot of questions," says Sabrina uncomfortably. She decides to change the subject. "How was school today?"

Sinclair is a fourth grade school teacher at an inner-city elementary school. He is the only male teacher in the entire building. As a college student he had claimed business as a major, but when his roommate had him read *Countering the Conspiracy to Destroy Black Boys*, his life and goals were changed forever. That most Black boys have never had a male elementary school teacher or seen a Black man read a book, write a letter, or compute a mathematical equation seemed a crime to Sinclair. He learned that the education of the majority of Black boys lies in the hands of White female teachers who, unable to handle or understand them, usually end up placing them in special education classes. He decided then and there to change his major to education.

"They sent two more boys to my class," says Sinclair. "I might as well be teaching special ed the way administration is constantly sending the problem cases to my room, especially the boys."

"They must send them to you because they know you can handle them," says Sabrina.

"That's sweet of you to say that, baby. I knew you cared for me." Sabrina giggles. "To tell the truth, though, I don't mind, because as long as they're in my class, they will not be labeled hyperactive or attention deficit disordered, and I surely won't recommend ritalin. The Board of Education is becoming as bad as the CIA and drug pushers."

"How'd you find the time to send me flowers, Sinclair? You've got your hands full during the day."

"I did it during my lunch hour when I was thinking about you."

"You are really sweet," says Sabrina.

"What do you plan to do for the rest of the evening?" asks Sinclair.

"Well, I'm going to get my nails done and buy some fish at Docks. What about you?"

"Grade papers, prepare my lesson plans for tomorrow, and spend the rest of the evening thinking about you."

"What comes to your mind when you think about me?" asks Sabrina.

"How fine you are," he says.

"What else?"

"I think about how I would like to have a future with you. I want us to have children together. I think about our parents getting together and them being happy as grandparents. I think about you visiting my classroom so that my boys can see my beautiful wife and how well I treat you.

Sabrina, do you ever think about me?" asks Sinclair. Sabrina doesn't say anything. "You don't have to answer that," says Sinclair, disappointed.

"Sinclair, I think of you as someone very special, very kind, and very caring. I think of you as the brother I never had."

"Brother?" asks Sinclair.

"Yes, brother. You can't get much closer than a brother."

"How about 'husband'?"

"That's true, but you want me to tell you the truth, don't you?" Sinclair doesn't answer. "Sinclair? Are you still there?"

"So, how's Doris doing?" he asks, changing the subject.

Sabrina is relieved. "Crazy as usual and always getting into my business."

"How long have you known Doris?"

"Close to ten years." There is another awkward silence.

"So, Sabrina, do you think that maybe we can get together over the weekend for dinner or a show?" asks Sinclair.

Sabrina wonders why she just can't tell this great guy yes. He's given her flowers, told her how much he loves her, he's not bad to look at—what was the matter with her? How could she prefer sex with someone like Tyrone over going out with a wonderful brother like Sinclair?

Taking a deep breath, Sabrina asks, "What movie do you want to see?"

"It really doesn't matter to me," says Sinclair, brightening. "I'd be happy watching videos, just as long as we spend some time together."

"That's sweet, Sinclair. I tell you what, let me see what's playing, and I'll leave a message on your answering machine tomorrow afternoon. Let me run before I'm late for my appointment. Don't be too hard on your children's school work."

"Okay, baby, love you," says Sinclair.

"Peace, my brother," says Sabrina.

Sinclair's supposed to be grading papers, but he can't concentrate. The conversation with Sabrina rolls around and around in his head. To many women, Sinclair is *all that*: 6'2", built like a long-distance runner (which he is), light skinned with curly hair. His gold, wire-rimmed glasses make him look like a hip intellectual. He stands up and looks at himself in the mirror. Is that the face of a brother? he asks himself. There's nothing sexy about being a brother. He tells the woman that he loves her, he sends her flowers and candy, and she calls him his brother. He wonders if his "sister" is going to call him back to confirm dinner and a movie for the weekend, or was she just blowing him off.

The following day, Sinclair is in rare classroom form. When it comes to his kids, not even his depression over Sabrina will get in the way of teaching. Standing at the blackboard, he tells the students to rise. "Alright, class, break up into your groups. I want the Ashanti, Ibo, and Zulus on this side and Hampton, Howard, and Tuskegee on this side. Practice your spelling words with each other until I tell you to stop. Then we'll have our quiz to see who's the best spelling team. Understood?"

"Yes!" says the children.

Sinclair has discovered that his children work better in groups, so he uses the peer group to reinforce learning. When he first started teaching he noticed that many high achievers were teased by their peers and it discouraged them. He took what appeared to be a negative and turned it around to make his classroom one of the most effective and enjoyable in the entire school. The increased noise and movement levels were a small price to pay for the impressive results proved by high classroom, state, and national test scores. The team approach encourages all students to carry their own load and the better spellers are valued, not put down, by their peers.

When the bell rings to signal the end of the day, a few boys lag behind. As usual, they beg Sinclair to take them home for the weekend. Only four of his twenty-one boys have fathers at home. He knows that they need more than just a male teacher; they need a daddy. But, as much as he would like to, he can't be a daddy to all of his students. He cracks a couple of jokes with them, then tells all to go straight home.

On his way out to the parking lot, Sinclair waves down Raynard, who's about to get into his red sports car. Raynard comes over and gives him the hand shake. "What's happening, man?"

"I'm just trying to keep my boys out of jail. If I can teach them how to read, I can keep them out of jail."

"I hear you. What're you doing this weekend?" asks Raynard.

"Well, I asked Sabrina out. I haven't heard from her, so my plans are up in the air right now," says Sinclair.

Raynard grabs Sinclair's shoulder and shakes him. "I keep trying to tell you, man, she's playing you."

"She wouldn't do that. She's been honest with me."

"Yeah, but does she keep the carrot dangling? Oh, baby, you so sweet. Oh, baby, you the man, but when it comes to getting down, she can't be found. She's playing you, man."

"Raynard, answer this question: I buy her flowers, run errands for her and her mother, call her every day, but it doesn't matter. What am I doing wrong?"

"I'll tell you what your problem is. You're too nice to these sisters and they take you for granted. They take advantage of you and violate your manhood. A Black man on a Friday evening needs to know what he's going to do and who he's going to do it with. He

92

should never allow a sister to put him in a holding pattern. That's where *we* need to keep *them* at. If they know you're waiting on them, they know they got the power. A man has got to have the power!

Now, I can tell you who I'm going to be with tonight and how long I'll let her stay in my bed. Right now, there are three sisters waiting on my phone call. Tell you what, after I make my choice, you can have your pick of the other two."

Sinclair shakes his head. "Man, you're scandalous."

"Look at you! She's got you shaking! Has she given you some? Is that why your nose is wide open because she opened up her legs to you?"

"You don't understand," says Sinclair.

"I got a minute, break it down to me. Explain how you lost the power."

Sinclair decided to shift the discussion. "Three women, Raynard? Why are three women necessary? Is it because you haven't found the right one? Isn't *quality* better than *quantity*?"

"No, man, I haven't found the right one, so in the meantime, three is better than zero."

"You got a point," says Sinclair.

"I know I got a point. You always gotta keep them wondering. You can't ever be predictable. You can't ever let them know how much you care about them because they'll take advantage of you."

"Man, I don't want to play games."

"Isn't she playing games with you? She's got you waiting on her phone call. She knows how you feel, but do you know how she feels? Do you know who she wants to be with tonight? This is not a game, it's war—war over power and control. Your problem, Sinclair, is that you make love with your heart and your head. I make love with my pipe."

"Your pipe can give you AIDS."

"Not the kid. My pipe is always covered. Why don't you hit on one of these fine sisters that's teaching in the building?" He waves to a group of women heading toward the parking lot. "Look at them! There are all kinds of sisters to choose from right here in this school. You're the only Black man with a classroom, you got status! You got your pick!"

"I never date anybody I work with 'cause the minute you break up with them, everybody'll know your business."

"That's a point there, but keep in mind what I told you—we're at war. It's about power!"

The two men shake hands. "Stay strong, Black man. Give me a call if you need one of mine for the weekend."

"Thanks, but no thanks," says Sinclair, slapping Raynard's hand.

On the drive home, Sinclair can't help but hope that Sabrina has left a message on his answering machine, despite what Raynard said about maintaining the power. As he opens the door to his downtown condominium, his first thought is of the answering machine. *Calm down!* he admonishes himself. Sinclair's condo is beautifully furnished with a white leather sofa, marble tile, African artwork on the walls, and books everywhere. He overlooks all of that as he walks straight into the bedroom to see if his answering machine is lit. It is, and he pushes the playback button.

It's his father, talking in that funny way of some older people who either feel uncomfortable with technology or just plain hate talking to answering machines. "Hello? Hello? Son, this is your dad. I just want to confirm that you will be at the health club at 10:00 tomorrow morning so we can see who can endure the longest on the treadmill and in the steam room. I'll see you then."

That is the one and only message. As much as Sinclair loves his father and is glad to know that he is being faithful to his workout routine, he is extremely disappointed that the message was not from Sabrina. It's 4:00 p.m., and she's had plenty of time to call him. Maybe she's going to surprise him and just come over. Maybe she got tied up at work. Maybe she was waiting until the evening edition of today's paper came out to check out the movie listings. Maybe Raynard was right, maybe he has lost his power and Sabrina was taking advantage.

Music, he needs music. He looks over his Toni, Anita, Maxwell, Fore Play, and Kenny G CD's and decides that he needs something a little stronger, like Yolanda Adams. Tonight may be a long night. Sinclair's probably the only Black man in the country spending time with Jesus on a Friday night rather than his woman. If there's such a male shortage, then why is he by himself? Raynard and brothers like him must be running a monopoly game on women. Trying to be positive, he breathes deeply and says aloud,

"Sabrina is going to call me. I know she loves me. She just doesn't know it yet."

Maybe he should call her, but what would he say? "Well, Sabrina, I just wanted to know if you've come to your decision yet about the show?" That sounds weak even to him. Maybe he should call just to see how she is doing. Maybe he should call to make sure that her telephone is working, that her car is working, and that she is not in some hospital. Maybe he should call Doris. Doris could help him understand Sabrina. He's only known her for six months, but Doris has known her for ten years.

Sinclair wonders about Raynard's women—are they pretty, are they smart? He imagines Raynard putting a bag over their faces when he takes them to bed, and it's a bet he doesn't call them the next day to express his feelings. Does he even remember their names? And who are these women sleeping with when they're not with him? The soothing, inspirational sounds of Yolanda Adams, Twinkie Clark, The Sounds of Blackness, Kirk Franklin, Dottie Peoples, and CeCe Winan help to calm his troubled soul.

As the darkness of night slowly descends upon his room like a warm blanket, reality dawns on

Sinclair. He's tried everything to make Sabrina love him, not as a brother, but the way a woman loves a man. He cannot escape the fact that Sabrina has never given any hint that she's interested in him. He finally goes to sleep, a deeply saddened but resolved man.

The next day on the treadmills, Sinclair decides to put the entire episode behind him and work off the heartbreak at the health club.

Sinclair's father, Jonathan Drake, is overweight and has high blood pressure. A mild heart attack earlier this year forced him to admit his mortality and commit to a change in lifestyle. Even Sinclair's mother, Leslie, has gotten into the act by learning how to cook her husband's favorite soul food dishes with less fat, salt, and no red meat.

"Are you ready to get your butt beat on this treadmill?" asks Mr. Drake.

"Don't even try it, Dad. You know I can run faster and longer than you can," says Sinclair.

Laughing, Mr. Drake says, "The young people of today! I'll teach you to respect your elders." Sinclair doubles over laughing. "Set your machine for thirty minutes, and we'll see who can last the longest."

Sinclair and his father go at it like two young boys in the park. Sweat drenches their bodies, and not even towels can keep them dry. They both endure to the end, and afterwards they walk around the track to cool down.

Later, in the steam room, Sinclair and his father enjoy the feeling of doing absolutely nothing. "Dad, you surprise me. For an old man, you hung in there pretty tough," says Sinclair, teasing.

"Yeah, and don't you ever forget it," he says, his eyes closed.

"Hey, Dad, I need some advice," says Sinclair.

"What's up, son?"

"Which one is better: to be nice or hard in relationships?"

"Woman problems, huh?" Sinclair nods his head miserably. "For as long as we've been married and before that, I have treated your mother like the queen she is. Ask her if you think I'm lying."

"Yeah, but Mom is one of a kind. They don't make women like Mom anymore."

"That's not true. Maybe you're just looking in the wrong places."

"To be honest, I don't look much at all. My whole life is teaching, working out here, and coming home."

"Well, what do you expect? That some fine honey's going to knock on your door and say 'trick or treat'?"

Sinclair laughs. "No."

"You gotta get out, and you gotta be patient, son. Most important, you have to believe the Lord is working on your mate right now."

"Dad, I think I found her in Sabrina. At least I did until last night."

"What happened last night?"

"It's a long story, but the bottom line is she looks at me as her brother, not her lover. She didn't call me back like she said she would."

Mr. Drake listens and nods his head sympathetically. "So what're you going to do?"

"I don't know, Dad. My *heart* wants to call her, but my *head* says I should wait for her to call me."

"After a few minutes in this steam room, maybe your head will melt and you'll make the right decision."

CHAPTER SIX

Kofi

This is an ocean of Black men, thinks Kofi, in awe of the miracle that's occurring all around him in Washington, DC. Never before in the history of America have so many brothers come together in the name of peace, reconciliation, and atonement. It is a powerful moment in time.

Kofi has been on his feet all day, but he wouldn't have missed this rich gathering for all the comfort and money in the world. He has always been committed to and worked for Black liberation, but the Million Man March is so much more. He feels that his very spirit has been touched. Never before has he shaken so many hands, hugged so many brothers, and shamelessly cried so many tears.

To say that today is the best day of his life is an understatement. Surrounded by so many brothers who love God, their history and culture, who can brush up against each other and step on each other's shoe without a violent response heals him on many different levels, and he knows he is not alone. In every brother's eyes is the spirit of love and harmony. Kofi clearly understands why he is at the Million Man March. It is not because of Minister Farrakhan or Rev. Jesse Jackson or Islam or Christianity. His participation is a bold stand against White supremacy. Most importantly, it is a stand for the empowerment of the Black male. The nationwide assault on Black men must end. As America builds fewer schools and factories and more and more prisons and stadiums, Black men must take radical action to reclaim their communities, their destiny.

Kofi did not fly to DC, nor did he take a bus. He *walked* for two days with a group of brothers from a halfway house in Philadelphia all the way to Washington, DC. Kofi is a member of the local organizing committee in Philadelphia, which was responsible for sending 200,000 brothers to the March. Kofi is on several subcommittees, including Drug Abuse and Education.

Kofi sees the March as a symbol of what is yet to come. The walk from Philadelphia to Washington demonstrated that Black men can do anything when they keep their eyes focused on God and if they are committed to the liberation of their people. Even though the Million Man March will not change the world overnight, it has motivated him to work with his local neighborhood school to infuse SETCLAE (Self-Esteem Through Culture Leads to Academic Excellence) into the social studies and language arts curriculum. The time has come to replace the Eurocentric curriculum with one that is rooted in an Africentric approach.

There are brothers as far as the eyes can see. The media can try and sell that lie about 400,000 brothers at the March, but all you have to do is trust your eyes, thinks Kofi. He is standing in an ocean of one million, maybe two million Black men. Kofi chuckles, thinking, if sisters ever wanted to find brothers, this is the best place in the world. Or as Dick Gregory said, "At least wives know where their husbands are!"

Some sisters were angry about not being included in the March, but many more were in total support. Kofi personally knew of sisters who pledged to stay home from work and White business establishments today. If only he could have received that kind of support from Andrea, his on-again, off-again girlfriend.

Late that night, he calls her as he promised he would. "Kofi! So you finally made it to DC. How do your legs feel?"

"Tired, but it's a good tired. Standing next to a million brothers takes your mind off the fatigue. Walking to DC I felt like Harriet Tubman escaping slavery through the Underground Railroad."

"I was looking for you on TV. They showed some of the brothers from the halfway house, but I didn't see you. Kofi, when are you coming home?"

"Probably tomorrow, but I won't be back to tutor until the end of the week. I'm trying to learn more about this SETCLAE curriculum because I think it'll be good for your school."

"Take your time. We appreciate what you and all the other men have done to give some direction to our youth," says Andrea.

"What did you do after school today?"

"Went home and watched the March."

"That's nice, but I wish you would have closed the school today."

"Not again! Can't we just agree to disagree on this one? Besides, it wasn't my decision. The board kept the schools open."

"How was attendance?"

"About forty percent of the students showed up."

"I'm glad that some people were conscious enough to keep their children home to honor the Day of Atonement. How many of your teachers were there?"

"About seventy-five percent."

"I'm not talking about White teachers. I expected all of them to be there. What percentage of *Black* teachers were there?"

"I would say about forty percent."

"I'm glad that sixty percent had enough sense to respect this holy day," says Kofi angrily.

"Kofi, can we change the subject?"

Kofi sighs loudly. "Okay, Andrea. Let's see. I think I probably lost five pounds from the walk and I really didn't eat much at the March. There were brothers selling bean pies and hoaggies, but I was too excited to eat. I'm getting hungry now, though. I need some chicken and greens. What about you?"

"I had some soup and salad just before you rang."

"So, do you feel differently now about the March?"

"What do you mean?"

"You gotta admit, you put us down. You didn't think anyone would show up."

"That's not true! You know that's not true. I just feel that the focus should be on the work that needs to be done at home, which means you've got to stay at home to get it done."

"I agree," says Kofi.

"Then why did you need to go?"

"I went because we needed to make a statement to America—that the Black man is back, that we're organized, that we believe in each other, that we can make a difference, that we can run a March of that magnitude and not seek any assistance from the White man."

"Tell me about this curriculum that you want to implement in my school."

"SETCLAE is an Africentric curriculum for kindergarten through twelfth grade. It has workbooks for students, a teacher's manual, thirty-two lesson plans, approximately one hundred supplemental books for children, and about twenty-five professional books for staff, in-service videos, posters, maps, certificates, and awards. Your staff can no longer complain about the lack of Black history lesson plans or teaching methods. This program appears to have it all."

"Kofi, I understand what you are trying to do, but these children are having a difficult time learning how to read. My eighth-graders cannot graduate unless they're reading at a sixth-grade level. So that's where my major focus is—on academics—not on the Black stuff."

Kofi pauses. Once again they have reached this impasse. At times he wonders why he likes Andrea. Why does he even put up with this woman? Because she looks good? Andrea has the body of an African woman, but the dead straight hair of a European. They look odd together—him with his wild dreadlocks and her with her relaxed hairstyles. How can he be so conscious and she be so apolitical?

"Maybe a major reason why Black children can't read is because they are not motivated by what they are reading. Don't you think that there could be some correlation among relevancy, the desire to learn, and achievement?"

"I won't deny that there's some merit to your argument, but I believe that the main reasons why our children don't learn are because they spend too much time watching television and listening to rap music and not enough time reading. I don't think the problem is *what* they are reading as much as the *lack* of reading all together. Marva Collins didn't become successful teaching her children how to read with Africentric material. She understands that future expectations and time on task are two essential ingredients to making any child successful."

"Why does it have to be either/or? We can have a relevant curriculum along with high expectations and time on task."

"Let's change the subject," says Andrea. "I don't want to argue with you. All we do is argue or, as you say, 'raise the level of contradictions.' We argue about which movie to see—*Sankofa* or *Independence Day*. Or how I should style my hair. You know,

Kofi, I don't like your locks, but I believe that you have a right to do what you want to with your hair, including not keeping it cleaned and combed. Kofi, whether you like it or not I have *good* hair and my mama and grandmama would be furious if I locked it. Be honest, one of the reasons why you like me is because of my hair. You like running your fingers through my *good* hair."

Kofi says, "Don't even go there, Andrea. I like you in spite of your *good* hair."

"Why don't you just date one of those 'in the struggle' sisters from the organizing committee?"

"Maybe I like you because of your fighting spirit. Maybe I believe that you have potential. Maybe I believe that at some point you are going to merge your tremendous intelligence and your underlying Blackness, and I want to be around to see this revolutionary change."

"That's not going to happen, Kofi. I'm Black and smart enough just the way that I am."

"Don't close your mind!"

"You just want me to be a copy of you!" Kofi sighs in frustration.

"Okay, Andrea, how about this: let's try not to argue. This weekend, let's get together and try to stay peaceful and loving with each other, okay?"

"I want the same thing," says Andrea, "but you know what's going to happen, Kofi. It'll be a nice weekend as long as we go to every Black speech and Black exhibit. I don't know if we've had one conversation since we met where we didn't talk about the plight of Black people. Sometimes, Kofi, I just want to be me. I don't want to talk Black or White. I just want to walk along the ocean. I want to look up at the sun. I want to throw rocks in the water. I want to lay a blanket out in the park. I want to play some nice music. I want to have a nice picnic. I want to play volleyball."

"I don't have a problem with any of that," says Kofi.

"Yeah, but we never do those things."

"I may want to do those things but, Andrea, there's no rest in this struggle. Black liberation is not about romance. Because I know that the CIA is putting drugs in our neighborhoods, it's hard for me to take time to play volleyball. Police are locking brothers up, shooting them in the back more than ever, so it's hard for me to look at the moon. Sisters on the street doing tricks for another hit, so it's hard for me to have a picnic. The children can barely read, so it's hard for me to take a walk on the beach."

"All I'm saying is that *for me,* there's a difference between my being your lover and my being your sister in the struggle. What you really want is for me to be a member of the local organizing committee."

"That would be nice," says Kofi. "I think it would teach you a few things about what's really going on in the community."

"I know more than you think I do! You're so arrogant, you think you're the only person who knows anything, or who cares. I am a principal of an inner-city elementary school, and even though you don't believe it, I'm trying to make a difference. I have to know what's going on." Andrea is so angry she is shaking. "Kofi, before we see each other again, I want you to think about what we're going to do this weekend and the rest of our lives.

"I'm tired of us jockeying back and forth on who's *Blacker* than who. I want a relationship with you, not some competition. I'm willing to accept you whether I agree or disagree with everything you do. The question is, Are you willing to accept me? Can you accept my perm, the fact that I may not bring SETCLAE into my school, and my desire to not go to every Black activity in town?"

"It's like that?" asks Kofi.

"And I'm not going to be on any local organizing committee!" Andrea says, nearly shouting.

"Are you giving me an ultimatum? Are you forcing me to choose between the liberation struggle and a relationship with you?"

"I never said that. I said, I'm willing to accept you—all of you. But can you accept me without trying to change me? Can you do some of the things that I want to do?"

"We can watch White movies. We can go to White restaurants. We can go to White stores. We can do *White stuff*," Kofi says sarcastically.

"So, it's just that funky attitude that makes me want to scream. Why does everything have to be Black and White? Why can't you just look at it as us going to nice stores and restaurants?"

Frustrated, Kofi says, "But who do you think is getting the money when you spend in those 'nice' restaurants and stores? Black people? Surely, you're not that naive!"

"I know who gets the money, but I can't change the world. I can try to enjoy the world as I find it. If you see negative all the time, that's what your life will be, negative. But if you look at things positively—"

"Andrea, I can't look at brothers getting smashed on the head day after day as a positive thing. It's—it's beyond my ability!

"You know, I don't understand sisters sometimes. On the one hand, you cry about Black men being irresponsible and not contributing to the uplift of the community. Stand up for us! Put these drug dealers in check! Spend some time tutoring and mentoring our boys! So I do these things, and all you can say is 'Too extreme. Too much. Lighten it up. Put a little milk in it.'"

"We definitely need more brothers like you who are doing good things in the community. There is no question about that. But at the end of the day, when the work has been done, can we spend quiet time? Just the two of us? Why can't you do both, work and play?"

"But I—" says Kofi.

"I'm not finished," says Andrea. Kofi lets her talk. "I don't want to go to Black restaurants all the time. The service is usually slow, the food is bad, and we always get interrupted by all the thousands of people you know. We're having some nice, intimate discussion and Joe Blow comes by wanting to talk about flyers for the rally or raising money or *whatever*. That gets on my last nerve, Kofi. When I go out to dinner with my man, I want him all to myself."

"Okay, Andrea, I hear you. I don't agree, but I hear you. Look, I'm exhausted. Talking to you has worn me out more than the walk to DC."

"Are you being cynical?"

"No, just trying to 'lighten up' as they say. And I'm really tired."

"Kofi, I want you to seriously think about this whole conversation, and before you call me again, I want you to think about whether you would be better off with a sister from the local organizing committee."

Kofi lies down, physically, emotionally, and mentally drained. Andrea is a good woman, committed to Black people in her own way, but he knows that it takes a certain type of woman to be married to a community activist, and he's not sure she could handle the demands.

Maybe Andrea is right. Maybe he would be better off with someone who is involved in the liberation struggle. Like the old-timers in church used to say, maybe he and Andrea are too unequally yoked. The goal should not be to change Andrea or anybody else, but to be with a sister whose values are already one with his.

Kofi is so exhausted that he sinks deeply into the mattress, dreadlocks wild about the pillows. Andrea's so fine, so smart, if only she was conscious, he thinks as he drifts off to sleep. Was wanting a fine, intelligent, and socially conscious sister too much to ask?

CHAPTER SEVEN
The Meeting

It's a perfect morning for a good workout, good weather for running cross country. The fall air is crisp and clear, and the leaves on the trees are full of orange, red, and brown flavors. David will work out today at Tommy's Gym in Hyde Park. It's Black-owned and attracts the more serious exercisers. And he loves the fact that there's a supervised child care facility with safe equipment for children.

David drops Junior off in the child care room and leaves him with a snack and a hug as he races to the locker room to change for a high energy aerobics class that's scheduled to start in a couple of minutes. There are about twenty-five participants (only three brothers), and Julie, one of the most well-built sisters David has ever seen, is leading the class. She *is* high-energy aerobics. It has been a humbling experience taking her class. David used to be like the brothers who look down on aerobics classes as being for sissies—until he took his first class with Julie. He couldn't even last fifteen minutes. But Julie was encouraging. She promised him that if he faithfully came to class and worked out two more times during the week that he'd be able to endure the full hour. He put her promise to the test and three years later, he's able to match her step for step and last the entire hour. In the process, he and Julie became good friends. At first he wanted more, but Tommy, the owner of the gym, saw her first. Tommy's a good brother, and David respects them both too much to try and break them up.

Randolph is also in Julie's class. He's gained a few more pounds since his days at Northwestern and he knows that exercise is the only way to get them off. He nods to David and winks at Julie. David wonders if he'll be able to last the hour.

Julie turns on Janet Jackson, and they do a fast warm-up to the heavy bass that is blasting through the gym. "Up and out, up and out, one, two, three, I say," shouts Julie in a mike attached to her headset. She looks like a rock star, and, at least for the brothers, the sight of her is worth the punishment she is putting their bodies through. David's learned to pace himself, but Randolph, having underestimated just how demanding aerobics is, goes full steam ahead. By the time Julie has moved the class to the high-energy segment, all Randolph can do is walk through the movements and flap his arms. David snickers. Another brother brought to his knees by Julie.

In the free weights room, Ron has set a goal of bench-pressing 420 pounds, nearly twice his weight. He stretches, then begins lifting, gradually adding more and more weight. At the 420-pound mark, he asks one of the brothers to spot him. He curls his hands around the bar and proceeds to lift the barbells for one set of ten reps. Several brothers are standing around, watching. "Way to go, brother Ron! Don't be so mean, Black man!" they encourage him. After the tenth rep, the brothers applaud. Ron is sweating and shaking, but manages to stand and take a bow.

Sinclair is in the freestyle room where there is a track, nautilus machines, treadmills, and bikes. He decides to depart from his usual thirty-minute run on the treadmill and give the Stairmaster a try. Sinclair is in excellent shape, but ten minutes into the workout he's sweating and panting. He endures to the end, and he vows to return. No machine will master him. He's training for the Olympics—at least the DuSable Museum's next runathon for sickle cell anemia research.

James inserts the pen in the eighty-pound bar of the abdominal machine. The love handles have got to go. Too much work and not enough exercise, that's the problem. What sister would want to deal with a workaholic entrepreneur with a gut? James joined the gym a few months ago, and he is beginning to see results, but he has a long way to go. He toys with the idea of putting the pin at ninety, but decides to go slowly. He doesn't need a sister that fast. He gets himself comfortable in the chair, grabs onto the two bars over his head, then begins to crunch twenty-five times. He stands and stretches, then does twenty-five more. His goal is to do two hundred reps, three times a week.

120

Kofi sets the treadmill at top speed in an uphill position. If he can walk from Philadelphia to Washington, he can run a treadmill routine. Many brothers in the liberation struggle ignore diet and exercise, but he refuses to neglect his body. The way he sees it, the movement needs marathon brothers with the stamina to fight for what's right. You can't do that if you're sick and tired. As Kofi runs on the treadmill, he imagines himself running through the bush in Africa. He's a warrior, fighting for his people. When he gets off, he has energy to spare.

Kofi's excellent physical conditioning allows him to participate in four walk a thons a year for Sickle Cell research, the United Negro College Fund, AIDS research, and the Stop the Violence project.

In the locker room, the brothers file in to change. Kofi nods to everyone and says, "What happening, ya'll?"

"Don't ask," says Randolph. He's sitting on a bench, towel over his shoulders, head thrown back against the lockers. "She tried to kill me, man." The brothers laugh.

"I'm surprised you lasted as long as you did," says David smugly. "You got to pace yourself, man."

Randolph groans, and their laughter echoes throughout the empty room.

David asks Sinclair, "So how was your workout? What did you do today?"

"Thirty minutes on the Stairmaster. How about you?"

"Julie was mean today. She was determined to make some people bow their heads." Randolph groans.

"But you finished, didn't you, bro'?" asks James.

"Yeah, but it was tough. Hey, I heard brother man pressed 420 today." Ron shrugs modestly. "The news was all over the gym."

"I just lifted some weights," says Ron. The brothers look at him with respect and vow to match him pound for pound.

The brothers drag themselves to the steam room, which happens to be empty. They spread out. It's *hot.*

"Think the Bulls will win the championship again?" asks Ron.

"I'm from the East Coast," says Kofi. "I got to go with New York."

"Black man, please. Shack and the Lakers will take it," says Sinclair.

"Houston's got Barkley, but what do I know?" says Randolph, half to himself.

"It's Chicago all the way," says Ron, "as long as they got Rodman on the boards. People don't understand that it's Rodman who makes the Bulls great, not just Jordan and Scottie. You got to get a strong brother like me on the boards who can do the dirty work. The Bulls never should have gotten rid of Horace Grant. That's why they lost that year. They didn't have a strong brother on the boards doing the dirty work. You can't win a championship if you don't have someone like Oakley, Grant, or Rodman doing the dirty work."

"I hear you," says Kofi. "How many of you made it to the March?"

"I was there. I took my son with me," says David. "It was powerful, man. I carried my son on my shoulders for twelve hours and didn't get tired because of the energy that was flowing from the brothers."

"I was there too. I had my Cub Scouts with me," says Ron, smiling. "Man, that was something."

"I took my boys with me, too," says Sinclair. "I teach fourth grade, and these bad boys needed to be there. It was good for them to see a million Black men being peaceful and positive."

James says, "I wasn't there physically, but I watched from my office the whole time. I run a business and it's difficult for me to get away."

Randolph is silent. "So what about you, bro'?" asks Kofi.

"I should have been there, man. I let the media influence me," he says honestly. "At the time I thought the March was about Farrakhan. I couldn't see any agenda or catch the vision. It's one of the big regrets of my life that I didn't go. If there's ever another March, count me in."

"It's all good," says Kofi. "It's all good."

"You know, a lot of the sisters were really mad about not being invited to come," says James. "Many of them resented doing 'kitchen work' in the local organizing committees."

"I heard some of that, but mostly I saw sisters supporting the March," says Kofi. "I was living in Philly at the time and worked on that committee. Some sisters fussed—in fact, the sister I was dating at the time didn't support it at all. I understood the desire to be a full participant, but I did not get my girl's attitude."

"She didn't support it at all?" asks Ron. The brothers shake their heads.

"She felt that a better approach was to stay at home and do the work. I tried to tell her that we had to make a statement and regroup our energies in order to come back home to do the work."

"Why couldn't it be about the March *and* doing the work at home?" asks Sinclair.

"I don't know, man, and that's why eventually we broke up. Too bad, too. Except for her close-mindedness, she was a good woman. She was even committed in her own way. She was the principal of an elementary school, and she loved those kids." There was genuine sadness in his voice.

"Yeah, that's the problem with Black women— we can't live without them," says Sinclair. The brothers groan. They've all been there. "Let me ask you all a question: How many brothers in the room are married?" They look around at each other. "No one?" They shake their heads. "Who's in a serious relationship that could lead to marriage?" No one responds.

Ron blurts out, "You mean nobody in here is involved in a serious relationship with a sister?"

"Well, I'm dating a woman, but I can't say that we've entered the serious relationship stage," says James. "We just met a couple of months ago."

"This is deep! Think about all the conversations you've had with brothers who brag constantly about women they're sleeping with, women chasing after them, women buying them things, and women calling them all night long.

"Have you heard this line from the brothers: 'Sisters are just like a bus. There is always another one coming'?" asks James.

"The one I hear all the time is 'If she don't give you what you want, you can always go across the street,'" says David.

"This *is* deep," says Sinclair. "Here are six strong, good-looking, intelligent Black men here and none of us are in a serious relationship! I need to call the sisterhood right now and tell them if they're looking for a good Black man just come into the steam room around 2:00 on a Saturday afternoon." The brothers laugh.

David asks, "How could this happen? Is anybody in here gay?" The brothers quickly shake their heads. "Are we all gainfully employed?" They nod their heads *yes*.

"Well, I don't know about the rest of ya'll," says Randolph, "but sisters just don't seem to appreciate the fact that I'm intelligent. When I was in school they used to tease me and call me a nerd because I couldn't dance or play basketball."

"You can't dance, man?" asks Ron mischievously. When Randolph winces, Ron holds up a hand. "I'm kidding, man. Being able to dance don't mean nothing. I love to dance, but I know that's not the measure of my manhood or my Blackness." Randolph nods his head.

David says quietly, "I had a good sister, the best. My wife died six years ago giving birth to my son. I'm ready to be in a relationship now, but what I'm finding is that the sisters can't deal with my son. There are plenty of sisters who want to date *me,* but I can't find a sister who wants to date *us.*" The brothers are silent. They deeply sympathize with the tragedy of David's loss.

Sinclair says, "I'm sorry to hear that about your wife, man. That must have really been tough. How did you get through that?"

David laughs and says, "Jesus *met* me at midnight. I was angry at Him, and I was hurting bad. I wanted to escape, but if you've ever been around children, you know they won't let you. So I have been walking with Jesus ever since she died."

"Praise the Lord!" say several brothers.

David shifts the discussion and asks Sinclair, "So what about you? How come the sisters haven't found you?"

Sinclair hesitates for a moment as he thinks about what Raynard said about him. He wonders what Sabrina is doing right now.

"Come on, man," says Kofi. "Give it up. How come the sisters haven't found you?"

"Well, the word on the street is that I'm too nice because I send sisters flowers and I tell them how I really feel. Sisters can't handle that, and they end up taking me for granted. 'I love you like a brother,' they'll say." Groans rise with the steam in the room.

"Not the brother bit," says Randolph. Sinclair is waiting for the usual "Dogg 'em. Take advantage" advice he gets from brothers like Raynard. To his surprise, there's silence. This is a different group of brothers, he thinks.

"Keep doing what you're doing, Sinclair," says David. "You don't want the kind of sister who likes game playing. Keep it real, and be patient. You just haven't found the right one."

"I don't know if I've found the right one or not," says James. "It takes a certain kind of sister to deal with an entrepreneur who works long hours and who rolls what money he does make back into the business. I meet a lot of sisters, but they want me to work nine to five at some company. They just don't understand that when a man doesn't pursue his vision, the relationship is going to suffer. He's going to resent the wife and the kids."

"That's the truth," says Kofi. "I need a woman to understand my commitment to the liberation struggle. I want to live Black! I want my home and my style of dress to reflect my culture."

Randolph blurts out, "So, I guess sisters think you're *too Black,* and they think that I'm *too White.*" The brothers laugh and high-five. "We got a group in the health club today!"

"What about you, brother," Kofi asks Ron. He has kept quiet about the sisters because their rejection of him is an embarrassment. He just shrugs.

"Come on, Ron. Get it out, bro," says Kofi.

"Well, my problem's complex."

"Yeah, so what else is new?" says James. Ron laughs despite himself.

"Alright!" says Ron. "The sisters I'm attracted to tend to be materialistic and status conscious. Even though I make good money at UPS, once they hear I'm a driver, they turn cold."

"I'll be damned!" says James. "They don't want me 'cause I left a good job, and they don't want you 'cause you kept a good job."

"Yeah, but not the right kind of good job. If I was an account exec at UPS, they'd like that. But driving a truck is blue-collar work," says Ron.

"It's gettin' kind a hot in here, ya'll," says Ron, the sweat pouring from every pore in his body, "and I think I'm about to pass out. Why don't we move this conversation into the shower?"

The water feels good on their bodies. It revives their energies and leaves them feeling refreshed.

"What's everybody doing tonight?" asks James, reluctant to let these kindred spirits disappear from his life. "Here we are, six Black men who are not in jail, not on drugs, and not gay. We are gainfully employed, handsome, intelligent, and in good shape (or getting there). Why don't we go to the Cotton Club tonight and show the sisters what good Black men look like?"

"That'll work," they say.

"Let me check on babysitting, but I don't think it'll be a problem," says David.

"I've been to clubs, but with no success," says Kofi. "Maybe tonight will be the night we'll meet some good sisters!"

CHAPTER EIGHT
At the Club

Tiffany, the owner of the Cotton Club, rushes James as soon as he enters the club. She gives him a big hug and kiss on the cheek.

"Lookin' good, Tiff," says James, winking at her. She is wearing black leather jeans, high heels, and a soft peach angora sweater.

"What brings you to the Cotton Club today, Mr. Entrepreneur who is always too busy to date or support other Black businesses?"

"Tiff, you know that is not true. I told you I'd come down to check you out. And I've invited five other brothers to meet me here. They should be pulling up any minute."

"Morehouse Men?" she asks playfully, thrusting out her chest in a poor but titillating imitation of a macho man.

"No, woman, I met these brothers at Tommy's Gym."

"Well, we've got a lot of action for you tonight. Jazz, dance music, a comedian, food, and lots of beautiful women, but don't try and make me jealous." James laughs at her.

Tiffany excuses herself for a moment to talk to her manager, and James takes note of what Tiffany has done with the place. "I'm proud of you," says James when she returns. Tiffany thanks him. "It's obvious you're not blowing all the money."

"Like I've always told you, James, I'm a business woman. I understand what it takes, personally and professionally, to make a business succeed." James nods.

"Entrepreneurship is more than just a notion," he says. "So, what's next for Tiffany Rawlings?"

"Don't you know?" she smiles as she openly shows her interest in him. Just then, Randolph and David walk into the club. They go on automatic and survey the club to get a read on the type of sisters who are here. James calls them over. They shake hands all around. In the presence of such fine, well-dressed men, Tiffany becomes even more animated, and the sisters in the house take notice, too.

Following close behind are Sinclair, Ron, and Kofi.

"Hotep," says Kofi.

"What does 'hotep' mean?" asks Randolph.

Kofi smiles at him. For some reason, even though they are so different, he likes this brother. "It means *peace*, my brother."

They shake and slap hands. They can feel the eyes of the sisters upon them, and it feels good. Ron says, "Sooky, sooky, now, where's the ladies room?" The brothers burst out laughing.

"I would like for you to meet the queen of this establishment, Tiffany Rawlings. Tiffany—Ron, Sinclair, David, Kofi, and Randolph," says James.

"Sorry, James, I know this is going to hurt, but I think I've just died and gone to heaven. Let me just stand here and breathe a moment." The club is filled with the sound of their heavy laughter which, when triggered by the flattery of a beautiful sister, is pure, raw, and sensual.

"I guess I can't monopolize you, the sisters will have my head, so go and circulate. The first round of drinks is on me."

"Thanks, babe," says James, kissing her on the cheek.

"Show your partners around, okay?" James nods. "I'll come and check on you later. Enjoy!"

Looking around, Kofi says, "My group should do a fund-raiser here." Kofi is a magnificent presence in his thick, long dreds and black neru shirt. His pants are long and loose. An Africa medallion made of pure gold boldly proclaims his love for the Motherland.

"Tiffany will set you up. Go for it," says James.

"Well, brothers, now that we're all here, let me walk you around and give you a tour of the great Cotton Club. Then we'll see if we can correct our problem tonight," says James.

They are welcomed onto the first floor by the sounds of R. Kelly, Mary J. Blige, and by the stares of elegantly dressed, beautiful Black sisters. These six fine Black men are hard to ignore and are a feast to the sisters' eyes. James leads them up the white staircase to the Green Room on the second floor.

"The comedy show starts at 10:30. Maybe we can check it out if we don't like what's goin' on the first floor," says James. They climb to the third floor, where there's a jazz combo playing. In the Gold Room, there's a brother playing saxophone.

"Who's that?" asks Ron, impressed.

"I don't know, man. Tiffany will often have local artists perform to give them exposure," says James.

"Man, that brother is *down*. I need to find out if he has a CD," says Ron.

"Let's ask Tiffany later. In the meantime I think we have some more pressing business," says James.

"I'm down for that," says Sinclair.

"Where to, gentlemen?" asks James.

"The ladies room!" says Ron. Randolph looks at him.

"Is there something you want to tell us, bro?"

"The best place to meet women is by the ladies room," says Ron.

The brothers are relieved that their friend is not some kind of pervert. "That's true. A sister will use the bathroom every half hour or so. We'll see all the sisters in the house eventually," says David. The brothers nod in agreement.

They position themselves at a table on the first floor by the ladies room. They are surrounded by a bubbling, tantalizing sea of beautiful Black sisters, and the brothers are definitely the center of attention. Toni Braxton is singing her latest hit.

A waitress takes their orders, and not even she is immune to their strong male presence. She can't resist flirting with them, even though it's against club policy.

Randolph and Kofi order orange juice, Ron, beer, and James, Sinclair, and David, white wine.

"I don't know about you, man, but this place reminds me of a meat market," says Sinclair. "Sisters look at us and we look at them. They think they know us and we think we know them. They think they can look at the way I'm dressed and tell where I work and how much I make. Whether I'm good husband material. On the other hand, if the sisters aren't fine, brothers won't dance with them."

"You know what I hate?" asks David. "When you ask a sister to dance and she says no. Just flat-out no. They need to wear a sign that says 'Leave me alone.'

I mean, sometimes I just want to dance. I'm not asking them to go to bed with me or marry me. I just want to dance."

"That's exactly what I'm talking about," says Ron. "They look at me and see a nice-looking brother. They're all interested until I tell them I work at UPS. They act as if I'm on welfare and am looking for a handout."

Tiffany comes by the table. "How's my favorite customers tonight?"

Kofi laughs and says, "We're just some good brothers looking for good sisters."

"Well, gentlemen, I'm glad you made it out tonight. *Mi casa es su casa*, okay?"

As Tiffany goes off to another table, Ron says, "That is one fine sister."

"Be careful about hooking up with an entrepreneur. The hours are long and there's not much time left for home life," says James.

"You ought to know, Black man," says Ron.

"What say we break up, navigate, and maneuver," says Randolph.

"Whoa," says David. "Do you know what you're looking for?"

"The same thing I've wanted since sixth grade—a fine sister with some brains!" says Randolph.

"I'm not asking for a lot. I just want a sister who is fine, smart, and likes children," says David.

"I want a sister who's a nine on a scale of ten," says James. The brothers chuckle. "Most important, I want a woman who will support me in my pursuit of financial self-sufficiency. She doesn't have to work in the business, but I need her to be in my corner. And, for a while, she's going to be on her own financially. I mean, I'll help her when I can, but she can't expect me to pay for everything all the time."

"Yeah, but you know how sisters are. They equate love with how much you spend on them," says Kofi.

"Well, most of my money is going into my accounting firm," he says firmly.

"I just want a woman who is fine and loves children, specifically my son," says David. "Sometimes sisters will say they love children and they want children, but when I introduce them to David Jr. they start stuttering. They say they want their own children, and are not interested in raising somebody else's."

"I want a sister who looks good. She can be an eight," says Kofi. "She's got to be down with the liberation struggle. Sisters who read romance novels by authors like Terry McMillan, Bebe Moore Campbell, or Connie Briscoe leave me cold. I need a sister who reads at least one consciousness-raising nonfiction book a year like *The Destruction of Black Civilization, The Isis Papers, Miseducation of the Negro,* or *Yurugu.* My woman celebrates Kwanzaa and lives the seven principles of Blackness. She wears African clothes, feels comfortable with her natural hair, and definitely likes my locks, because I'm not getting rid of them. I need a sister who is fully involved in the liberation struggle and understands the meaning of that commitment."

"You may have to go to Africa to find that sister," says Randolph. Kofi shoots an intense look at him and then realizes that he might be right.

"Kofi, I would like for you to talk to the boys in my class. I talk to them all the time about the conspiracy to destroy Black boys, but they might really believe it coming from you," says Sinclair. "By the way, who is the author of *Yurugu?*"

"Marimba Ani," says Kofi. "If you ever wondered about the origins of the Eurocentric mindset, that's the book to read. It ain't easy reading, though, bro'."

"That's cool. I'm up for the challenge," says Sinclair. "What else do I have to do in the evenings but grade papers and read."

"Oh, man, it can't be that bad," says James.

"Man, if you only knew. I need a beautiful sister, too, but most important to me, she can't be into playing games. Later for that. I'm not into trying to control a woman or dogg her out. I want to be nice. Being nice to a woman turns me on. I need a sister who'll respond to my kindness by loving me back. My kindness is not a weakness, it's my strength." The brothers nod in understanding and as they talk, it dawns on them that it may be difficult finding a "real" sister in the Cotton Club.

"I want my woman to be finer than fine. She's got to be able to turn some heads, and she's got to be able to cook—or at least be willing to learn," says Ron. "But I want her to be real, too, not materialistic or status conscious. Some sisters have become married to their careers. I see UPS as a job. I don't dream about it at night. It doesn't affect me over the weekend. I go in, work hard, do my eight hours, and I'm through with it. I'm not like you, James. It's just a job to me. I just want a fine sister, good meals, a clean house, and sex at least three nights a week."

"Only three?" laughs David.

"Maybe seven," he says, grinning, and they whoop and slap him on the back.

"Black man!"

Randolph waves to get their attention. "My woman doesn't have to be fine to other men, just to me. I don't want a bear, but a seven would be cool. My first requirement is intelligence and a love of culture. I'm looking for a sister who likes to read, visit museums, art exhibits, multicultural activities, lecture series, and is comfortable in cyberspace."

"You don't want a bimbo," says Sinclair. "That's valid."

"I guess you could say that I'm looking for an intellectual. Stimulating dialogue turns me on, and she doesn't have to agree with me either. In fact, if she has the ability to change my mind about things, I would lay down my life for her."

"You're a deep brother," says Kofi with respect.

"Man, life is just one big party to our people. Too many of us seem to have no interest in the serious issues—environment, ecology, abortion, the national deficit, nuclear arms, or foreign affairs. These are not White issues, they affect us all." Kofi nods. "Man, I wouldn't have a problem reading *Yurugu*, but I would suggest you read Alan Greenspan, Ralph Nader, and Studs Terkel."

"Now that we all know what we want, I got to make a move on that fine sister in the black pants and red blouse who has been looking at me all night," says Ron.

"Go for it, brother," they say.

Suavely, Ron walks over to the table and extends his hand. They go out on the dance floor to finish off Baby Face. Toni Braxton's latest slow song begins, and Ron draws her close to him. "I've been check'n you out all night. What's your name?"

"Daphne, and I didn't think you noticed me. I was beginning to think you and your friends were gay," she says.

"Do I look gay? Do I act gay?" asks Ron.

Daphne lets her hands slowly linger over his arms and chest. They are both enjoying the sensuality of her touch as Daphne looks into his eyes and says, "Well, you can't always judge a book by its cover."

They continue to move closer to each other as they dance to the tune of Maxwell.

"Do you come to the club often?" asks Ron.

"This is only my second time. I'm on the road a lot. I'm a buyer for Lord & Taylor," she says. Ron stiffens slightly. And she was so pretty, too. "So what line of work are you in?" Her voice is soft and sweet in his ear.

"I'm a driver for UPS," says Ron flatly.

"Oh, that's nice," says Daphne, moving back ever so slightly.

Baby Face ends, and Ron escorts Daphne back to her chair with no further conversation. He walks back to his table.

"So how was she?" asks Sinclair.

"The usual—fine, accomplished, and intelligent. She's a buyer for Lord & Taylor, and she travels a lot. I think we could have had a future together if I had said I was an account executive for UPS," says Ron.

Sinclair has been exchanging strong eye contact with a medium tan female dressed in a canary yellow pants suit. She's sitting at a table with two other sisters. Sinclair has determined that she is the finest sister at the table if not in the club.

"I wish they made brothers like they used to with manners. Remember when brothers would buy you a drink and come to the table and ask you to dance?" said one sister. "I do remember that back in the 1800's there was a real type of chivalry. Brothers did not allow sisters to dance with each other, but now they want us to *ask them* and they have the gall to think that this lack of romance would lead us to some hot action at the end of the evening. "Look, I just came to have a good time. I just want to dance." said another sister.

The waitress comes over to their table and gives Belinda a note and points to Sinclair. Belinda silently reads the note. I would like to buy you the drink of your choice. All I ask in return is a few minutes of your time. Let's talk at the bar.

"What does it say girl?" chimes her friends.

For a moment, Belinda ignores them, then says, "eat your heart out." She looks at Sinclair very sensual and walks over to the bar.

James warns Sinclair not to let her take all of his money. David hollers to Sinclair as he is walking to the bar, "tell her to introduce us to her friends."

"Thank you for responding to my note. My name is Sinclair."

She smiles and says, "my name is Belinda. Why did you send the note to me and is that your standard modus operandi?"

"I don't go to clubs often and I thought it was a shame for me to see someone so beautiful and not be able to talk with her." This triggers an obvious blush from Belinda.

"What brought you out to the Cotton Club tonight?"

"You will never believe this, but the brothers at my table are single, and we met today at Tommy's health club and found we had a lot in common." Belinda looks curiously at Sinclair and then at his table.

"You mean nobody is married, living with anyone, gay, or hooked up with some White girl?"

"Nope. Are you surprised? Haven't you seen six good brothers together before?" he asks.

"What makes you good?" asked Belinda teasingly as she softly bats her eyes.

"I could answer that question," said Sinclair "but why don't you give me *your* definition of a good brother."

"I asked you first," said Belinda.

The bartender approaches them and asks, "What would you like? Belinda says a virgin pina colada and Sinclair orders a glass of white wine.

Belinda says, "okay. I'll answer first since you sent me the note. A good brother is kind, buys his lady a drink, sends her flowers, cards, candies, and does not play games. He calls and writes notes letting her know how he feels. A good brother is faithful."

Sinclair smiles and says, "you just described me to a tee."

Belinda shrugs it off and says, "that's what all the brothers say. But talk'n the talk and walk'n the walk are two different things. Brothers and sisters do a great job of hooking up, but our divorce rate is pathetic, which says something about our lack of commitment."

"How would you respond if a brother did all that

you described, and more? Would you play him for being weak? Would you take him for granted? Would you view him as your brother or your lover?" asked Sinclair.

"Whoa! You're asking a lot of questions. Is this confessional? Are we making this personal? Is that your baggage?" asked Belinda.

"Belinda just answer the question," said Sinclair.

"How did I respond to your note? Why don't you send me more notes, cards, flowers and candy and see how I will respond?" asked Belinda.

Her two girlfriends come over to the bar and tell Belinda they're going up to the comedy club. Belinda introduces Sinclair to them and asks whether he and his good brothers would like to check out the show. Sinclair leaves them for a moment and goes over to his table.

"Things are looking good tonight. I knew I had good taste. Belinda invited you to go up to the comedy club with her girlfriends. Three of you are going to have to find someone upstairs, or we can all sit together," says Sinclair.

Randolph says, "I'm for check'n out the show;

let's all sit together. I don't need a lady to laugh."

They all walk up the winding staircase to the comedy club, which generates snickering as the brothers take-in the view of the sisters from the rear. The show will begin in five minutes, and while they're waiting, Sinclair and Belinda coordinate the introductions with Tina and Marie.

Tiffany goes on to say, "I'd like to welcome you to the Cotton Club. Tonight we have a special guest who is a dear friend of mine. He knew I could not afford him, but we grew up together and he has never forgotten his roots. His only requests were that his name not be advertised so that the crowd could be manageable and that he would only perform for twenty minutes. I present to you my fourth grade boyfriend hot off HBO Def Comedy Jam, Tyrone!"

The crowd is amazed and they stand on their feet and give him a five minute standing ovation.

"Tiffany didn't mention that she broke up with me in the fourth grade. See, I used to sit behind her in class and she wore her hair in these two long pony tails. One day I decided to help her mama out, so I shortened them for her. You know I'm tall today

because her father lifted me two feet off the ground."
The crowd bursts into laughter.

"Sisters don't ever ask me where are the brothers? Did you see the Million Man March? I have never seen that many brothers together to do anything. Those brothers understood it was not about Farrakhan or Jesse. When the police pull me over at 3:00 in the morning, they don't ask me am I a Muslim or Christian, a Q or an Alpha, a Democrat or Republican. They just see a nigger to beat.

I pray it never happens to me, but if it does Lord please send me a White man with a camera or tape recorder like you did for Rodney King and against Texaco." The audience hollers.

"Have you ever read or responded to those classified ads about finding a mate. I wrote this one sister who said she was beautiful inside and out. I met her at a restaurant and she was so ugly that I just couldn't stay around long enough to view her insides." The audience by now is hysterical.

"One ad said she likes to travel, attend concerts, plays, and have romantic dinners. I like all that too, but who's paying for it? Who wouldn't like to travel to Hawaii or cruise along the Caribbean and the Nile at my expense? Next time you write that ad let me know how much you're putting up." James is cracking up and almost falls on the floor.

"I speak at a lot of colleges. I often ask the students what is the female to male ratio on campus. (Sisters love to try to convince me that we have this tremendous male shortage.) When I spoke at Hampton University they said it was 8:1. I knew they were exaggerating so I called the admissions office and out of 4500 Undergraduate students, 1800 were males and 2700 females. I'm not good with math, but that doesn't sound like 8:1. I spoke at Alabama State and they said it was 12:1. The admissions office said they also had 4500 students, 2500 females and 2000 males. Lastly, when I spoke at Clark University, they said the ratio was 14:1. Admissions said they had 4400 students, 3100 females and 1300 males. Repeat after me. Perception may not be reality. Keep it Real, I'm out of here. Peace! The crowd gives Tyrone another standing ovation.

Sinclair and Belinda ultimately exchange telephone numbers and he promises that he's going to show her he's a good brother, and Belinda reminds him that the proof is in the walk, not the talk.

"Well, it's getting late for me," says David, "but before I go, I'm inviting everybody to Calvary Baptist Church tomorrow for the 11:00 a.m. service. There are a lot of good sisters there."

"I don't do church, bro," says Kofi. "I haven't been to church since I moved out of my parents' house. Does your church have a White image of Jesus Christ in the sanctuary?"

"No," says David. "I think you'd approve of the images."

"I don't know either," says James. "All the preachers want is your money. These economic pimps, they couldn't run a real business to save their lives, so they start a church and beg for your money. I don't see much difference between a brother begging for money on the street and a pastor begging for money in the pulpit. They even have the nerve to get uptight when you ask them for an income statement or a balance sheet. Most of them don't even know what they are."

"Marx said that religion is the opiate of the masses," says Randolph. "You have pastors with a ninth-grade education leading the masses. I left the

church a long time ago because it was not intellec-
tually stimulating. It's hard for me to understand
how someone was born of a virgin, died, and then
rose three days later. I've been waiting for someone
to scientifically explain that."

"Well, we know the Cotton Club doesn't work
for all of us," says Ron. "Maybe we'll find some good
sisters tomorrow at Calvary."

"Let's do it," says Sinclair. "Let's meet up at
10:45 and finish off the weekend with something
positive."

"Okay," say the other brothers—some more
excited than others.

CHAPTER NINE
Finding Some Good Sisters

"Have I missed anything?" asks James. An usher in blue and white smiles and hands him and the other brothers a church bulletin. They walk over by David who is standing in the foyer. David and Junior were the first to arrive.

"They just began praise and worship," says David. Junior wants to ask his father a thousand questions: "Who is that man? What's he doing here? Where do you know him from, Daddy?" David puts a finger to his lips to quiet him before he gets started. Junior usually sings in the youth choir, but David wants him by his side today.

"Where's Kofi?" asks James.

"I don't know. If the brother doesn't show soon, we're going in. I don't want to miss a blessing," says David. "When was the last time you all were in church?"

"Easter," says James.

"About six months ago," says Randolph.

"I try to make it once a month, usually on communion Sunday," says Sinclair.

"I try to make it every Sunday," says Ron.

Kofi makes a dramatic entrance wearing a maroon neru suit with his gold African medallion. "Sorry I'm late, brothers. It was hard getting up this morning." They understand how it is.

"I'm just glad you made it," whispers David. "Let's go in and catch the last part of praise and worship."

The brothers turn heads as they walk down the aisle. They find some seats together in a middle pew. There are approximately 300 members in the church, most of whom are female. The sisters feast on the vision of so many fine Black men in their church. "Praise the Lord! Hallelujah!" they say with more enthusiasm and gratitude. In fact, the church becomes a single pulse of joy and praise. Arms are thrown high in the air and clapping begins. It swells to a thunderous roar. Ron and David are comfortable with this style of worship, but the others are not. They stand with the rest, though, and try and participate as best they can. Kofi looks around the walls of the church for any signs of a White Jesus, but doesn't see any. Behind the pulpit is a stained glass window with a beautiful depiction of the African Christ.

"This is the first time I've seen the correct image of Christ in a church," says Kofi.

David whispers, "Doesn't the Bible say He had hair the texture of wool and feet the color of bronze?"

"Right, but too many of our churches still have White, blonde images of Jesus, then they want to say that color doesn't make a difference. If we are to worship Him in spirit and *truth*, then make him African!" says Kofi.

They sing "Order My Steps" followed by "Shake the Devil Off." It's like a party in the church with everyone singing, clapping, and swaying with the praise team.

"I don't know about you, but I came to praise His name this Sunday morning! We're gonna have a Jesus party up in here today!" says the team leader. The processional begins, and the pastors and choir march down the aisle to "We Have Come Into This House to Worship Him."

Pastors David and Naomi Solomon are both tall and regal looking in their kente robes. Their two children sing in the youth choir.

Following the pastors are fifty children, from age five to thirteen, singing to the top of their lungs. Even Kofi is moved by their rousing rendition of the gospel staple, and he heartily approves of their orange-checkered dashiki uniforms.

Kofi leans over to David. "How is Naomi allowed to be a pastor when women are supposed to be silent in the church?"

David laughs. "You can't hold the tongue of a good sister who's on fire for the Lord, brother!" Kofi smiles. "We have sisters who sit on the deacon board, too. They are fully involved with collecting the offerings and on communion Sunday, they distribute the sacraments." David writes a note to Kofi, "Read Romans 16 and Galatians 3."

Pastor Naomi walks to the pulpit and gestures with her hands for everyone to stand as she leads them in singing the Lord's Prayer. After the song, Pastor David asks all the visitors to stand. There are nine visitors, including an elderly couple who are visiting their brother and two middle-aged sisters visiting their daughters. Each visitor is asked to tell their name and a little bit about themselves. David can feel the eyes of 200 women upon them.

"My name is Randolph Brown. I'm an engineer with Motorola and I'm here as a guest of David Johnson."

"My name is Sinclair Drake. I'm an elementary school teacher and I'm also here visiting my friend David Johnson."

"My name is Ron Brooks. I work with UPS and I'm with my friend David Johnson."

"My name is James Robinson. I own an accounting firm, and I'm with David Johnson."

"My name is Kofi Mahiri. I'm a social worker, community activist, and a coordinator of the local organizing committee for the Million Man March, and I'm also visiting my friend David Johnson."

"Welcome to all of our visitors. Here at Calvary Baptist Church, visitors are always welcome. We hope that there will be some song, prayer, or word that will touch your heart. If you have not already confessed that Jesus Christ is Lord, we pray that you will give your heart to Jesus on this day. After service our members will greet you at the visitors' section, because we truly appreciate your taking time out of your busy week to spend time with us. May God Bless! You can take your seats. We will now have the announcements read by Sister Gloria."

Sister Gloria walks toward a smaller podium and speaks clearly into a microphone. The congregation gives her a round of applause. "We would like to encourage all of you to read the bulletin in its entirety, because today, I'll just be giving you the highlights of the major events for the upcoming week. Men's Bible Study will be on Monday night. We're reviewing *Adam! Where Are You? Why Most Black Men Don't Go to Church*. On Tuesday is women's Bible study. We'll be reviewing *Woman Thou Art Loosed!*

"The Food Pantry is open on Wednesday from noon to 2:00. Volunteers are still needed to serve approximately 500 families in the neighborhood. We also need volunteers for our after-school tutorial program and Black History classes. Classes are held Monday-Thursday from 4:00 p.m. to 6:00 p.m. Rites of Passage for boys and girls between eleven and sixteen years of age is on Saturdays from 2:00 p.m. to 4:00 p.m. The Credit Union will be opened after service to process any transactions. The Loan Committee is asked to meet briefly after service.

"The Singles Ministry has an exciting event that they are planning next Saturday, a health club extravaganza! We have rented Tommy's Gym in Hyde Park, which is an African American owned and operated facility. There'll be volleyball, basketball, swim, aerobics, and more. There will also be a buffet of delicious, nutritious dishes from 6:00 p.m. until 12:00 p.m. We hope to see everyone there. May God bless you on this Sunday," says Sister Gloria, finishing the announcements.

The choir then sings "I Know That He's Real" and "I'm a Witness." Several people in the congregation catch the fire of the Holy Spirit, and they take to the aisles to dance. Kofi and Randolph look at each other for reassurance. They can't imagine what on earth would move them to let loose like that.

Following the two selections, Pastor David has all the children, including those in the choir, to come down around the altar for Children's Hour. Junior joins the energetic crowd at the pastor's feet. They still themselves, though, when he begins to speak. He teaches them the story of the chicken and the eagle. Junior turns and smiles at his father. It's his favorite story! David motions for him to turn back around. Sinclair knows the story, too, and wishes that he could have told it. The pastor tells the children that they are wonderfully made and that God did not make a mistake when he made them. If God had wanted them to be chickens He would have done that. The Pastor tells them that God wants them to soar, fly, make the honor roll, and grow to their full potential.

The children return to their seats, then Pastor David readies the congregation for prayer. A hushed reverence fills the sanctuary with a peace that greatly moves the brothers. David is reminded of the peace that passes all understanding. Pastor David invites those in need of prayer to come to the altar. The organist plays a solemn, slowly paced song. David walks down the aisle to the altar, holding his son's hand. The other five choose to stay behind. Everyone is told to hold hands and secure the name of the person sitting next to them. The pastor then leads them in the altar call.

While the prayer is being given, David thinks about the tragedy of losing his wife during the birth of his son. Randolph and Kofi can't imagine the God to whom they are praying. It is difficult for Randolph to pray to someone he cannot see. Kofi still visualizes a White Jesus, so from time to time he opens his eyes and looks at the Black Jesus behind the pulpit. As the prayer concludes and everyone goes back to their seats, David is wiping the tears from his eyes as he sits next to Kofi and Randolph. They don't know if they should hug him or hold his hand so they do nothing.

Pastor David then has the ushers come forward to collect the tithes and offerings. A special offering will also be collected by the deacons. The money will go to scholarships for deserving youth in the church and also to the United Negro College Fund. The ushers are efficient and courteous, and the brothers appreciate how this portion of the service is conducted. This is serious business, and there is no feeling of hype, salesmanship, or coercion. Kofi and Randolph decide they will give to the second offering.

It is time for the sermon to begin, and this Sunday, the congregation will have the pleasure of receiving the Word from Pastor Naomi. She has the congregation read with her from Genesis (2:18 and 24). David, Sinclair, and Ron brought their Bibles, which they share with Kofi, James, and Randolph. "And the Lord God said, It is not good that man should be alone. I will make him a helper comparable to him. Verse 24 says, 'Therefore, a man shall leave his father and mother, and be joined to his wife, and they shall become one flesh.'"

"Our New Testament scripture is Second Corinthians 6:14." Pages fly quickly throughout the congregation. Sinclair and Ron take a little longer, but they eventually find the passage. 'Do not be unequally yoked together with unbelievers for what fellowship has righteousness with lawlessness and what communion has light with darkness.' Today's sermon is titled, 'God's Formula for Marriage,'" says

164

Pastor Naomi, and the entire church says, "Amen." Marriage and love relationships are favorite topics, so the anticipation for a good message is high. The members also know that Pastor Naomi has keen insight in this area.

"In the book of Genesis, God says that He was pleased when He made the earth, but there was one problem: Adam was not happy. Adam was not happy because Adam was made *incomplete*. You see, the Lord made us needy. Man was not made to live alone, so God created woman. Verse 23 says that "This is now bone of my bone and flesh of my flesh. She shall be called 'woman,' for she was taken out of man.

"What man needed he had all along! What woman needed she had all along! What we have been trying to find *outside* of ourselves has been *within* us all along. The Lord made us needy. Turn to your neighbor and say, 'The Lord made us needy.'"

The brothers tell each other, "The Lord made us needy." Then they slap high-fives all around because they know she is so right.

"God's math is different from what we are taught in school," says Pastor Naomi. "In verse 24 it says, 'For this reason a man will leave his father and mother and be united to his wife, and they will become one flesh.' In school, weren't you taught that one-half plus one-half equals one whole? And weren't you taught that one plus one equals two?" The congregation nods and shouts a chorus of "Amen" and "Preach!"

"But see, that's man's math," she says, getting excited. "Remember what Paul said in First Corinthians: "God's thoughts are not our thoughts." His math is not our math, because in verse 24, the Lord teaches us that one plus one equals one." There is a great outburst from the congregation. The sisters in particular wave their arms in the air. Kofi and Randolph smile knowingly. Oneness in God is something to shout about. "People come to me and my husband all the time whining and crying that they can't find a good mate. They want a mate that will make them happy. We have to constantly remind folk that the best person to be married to is someone who is *happily singled.* Turn to your neighbor and say 'happily singled.'" The brothers say it to each other, but they lack conviction. They don't *feel* happily singled.

"If you are expecting someone else to make you happy, you're going to have problems. First of all, only God can make you happy. Folks claim they want a divorce because their spouse did not make them happy, but the problem with most marriages today is that you got two halves not making a whole. They think that one-half plus one-half will equal one, but in God's math, one-half plus one-half equals one-half!"

"Preach!" shouts the congregation. "Go 'head, Pastor!"

"Two halves do not make a whole, there is still something missing. Had they been equally yoked, as we read in Second Corinthians, had they been believers, had they had a right relationship with God, they would no longer have been a *half*. They would have been *whole*."

The church is on its feet. "Preach, Pastor, preach!"

"People who are incomplete wouldn't know a good mate if one dropped out of the sky and landed on their porch with a sign that said "Mate from Heaven."" The people whoop and shout "Hallelujah!" and "Glory be to God!"

"Brothers and sisters, the best way to develop a relationship is to first develop a relationship with God, then you can develop a relationship with your spouse.

"And another thing! I know sisters who have pity parties all night long about the male shortage. All you hear 'em talk about is two to one, three to one, five to one. There you go again, looking at it from man's perspective. The media loves to remind us that all brothers are either in jail, on drugs, unemployed, or homosexual. Talking about he's almost extinct like he's some kind of animal! But this is what God has to say to you, Black women. How many men are you looking for? What do you care about the odds? All you need is ONE!"

"Thank you!" shout the sisters, waving their arms and stomping their feet.

"The problem for many of our sisters is that because they compromise and stay with a half rather than developing themselves to be whole, they end up sleeping with a half, or should I say a piece of a man, and miss the blessing that God is preparing for them right now with a whole man. How can you be available for the whole man that God is preparing for you if you are shacking and compromising with half a man?

"And when we talk about being equally yoked, brothers also need to understand what is being said. God's formula for a relationship is to look at the heart. Man looks at the outside—read Second Samuel—but God looks at the heart. Almost every study that I've read on relationships indicates that brothers rank beauty first. Don't get comfortable, sisters, because research shows you value the checkbook." The congregation laughs. "But, brothers, be honest. Do you look at the outside or do you look at the inside? You could have missed your blessing because you only looked at the outside while the Lord had prepared a jewel for you on the inside. I know from my counseling that a pretty face and legs, some chest and butt can't keep a marriage together for forty years. It's going to take more than that. Being equally yoked is not about beauty. It's about creating and maintaining a bond. It's about friendship. It's about sharing the same faith—that Jesus Christ is Lord. It's about a good man's steps being ordered by the Lord."

James knows that he is guilty of looking on the outside. But does being equally yoked mean finding someone who also wants to be an entrepreneur or finding someone who believes in Jesus?

Randolph thinks if he found a woman who believed in Jesus, they'd be unequally yoked because he doesn't have the faith.

Thinking about God's math makes Sinclair realize that he's been acting like half a man. When Sabrina did not call that night, he surely didn't feel happily singled. In fact, her lack of interest made him miserably depressed.

Ron thinks about the fact that he failed to mention earlier in the service that he is a truck driver for UPS. Why was he not completely honest in the house of the Lord? Doesn't the Lord love him just as he is, and why should it matter to him what sisters think?

Being equally yoked for Kofi means finding a sister who is going to be as committed as he is to the liberation of African people. But he must admit, he too has been guilty of looking at a woman's body first.

Pastor Naomi opens up the doors of the church. She asks, "Do you want to be happy? Do you want peace? Do you want joy? The Lord made you needy and not just needy for each other. The Lord made you needy for Him. Is there anyone here who wants to be saved? Is there anyone here who wants to join Calvary Church?" Sinclair has heard those questions before, but he has never walked the aisle. Maybe he'll do it on Communion Sunday at the church he's been visiting lately.

Kofi, James, and Randolph know they aren't ready. They have no desire to walk the aisle, but they enjoyed the service and may even come back. Three people accept salvation and join the church—a mother and her son and a middle-aged Black male. The choir sings "Amazing Grace," and Pastor David ends the service with a prayer and a request that visitors adjourn to Fellowship Hall.

David teases his friends and says, "Now don't start taking phone numbers and remember what you heard in the sermon. Don't just look at how fine the sisters are. Try to look at the heart."

"We heard the sister," laughs Kofi.

"Loud and clear," says James.

"I think I'd like to go to that singles party at the gym," says Ron. They agree to make that their next outing.

As visitors, the brothers are treated like honored guests and members of the church family. Everyone shakes their hands and tells them how wonderful it's been to see such fine Black men in their church. The pastors personally speak to each of them and invites them back. The women members are at first discreet, but as there is a lot of laughing and joking and genuine fellowship, they begin to approach them more boldly, mostly asking them if they'll be attending the singles event.

The brothers are in heaven. They try to remind themselves about the message they just heard, but the sisters are so beautiful they can't help but cast appreciative glances. Why can't they have women who are as beautiful on the outside as they are on the inside? Old habits die hard, but each sister— from the darkest to the lightest, the heaviest to the thinnest—each has her own special beauty.

The brothers are grinning from ear to ear. A sister asks David, "Where did you find them? Are you going to bring them back?" David doesn't know what to say, because he doesn't know. But he does know that *this could be the best place to find a good sister.*

As he looks over at the sisters he also knows that *this could be the best place for them to find a good brother.*

A Sister's Response

I spend a lot of time talking to my sisters, and in between raising our children and earning our livings and struggling for our freedom and loving our womenfriends and building a new world, we *sometimes*—every now and then—talk about the brothers. I think it is time we put forward a working definition of who and what we are looking for.

- We are looking for a good brother.
- We are looking for a righteous brother. A *real* righteous brother.
- An all grown up, ain't scared of nuthin', and knows it's time to save the race righteous brother.
- A good father/good husband/ good lover/good worker/good warrior/serious revolutionary brother.
- A tuck the baby in at night and accept equal responsibility for child raising and household maintenance chores righteous brother.
- A generate a regular check righteous brother.
- A love black women, protect black children and never hit a woman righteous brother.
- A turn the TV off and let's talk instead righteous brother.
- A turn the TV off and let's make love instead righteous brother.
- A stay at home 'cause that's where you wanna be righteous brother.
- A brother who can listen.
- A brother who can teach.
- A brother who can change. For the better.
- We are looking for a righteous brother. What we used to call *a good brother.*

Pearl Cleage | *Deals with the Devil: And Other Reasons to Riot* Reprinted by permission of Ballantine Books.

NOTES

NOTES

NOTES

NOTES

NOTES

NOTES

NOTES